(SEM)EROTICS
Theorizing Lesbian : Writing

Editorial Board

The Cutting Edge:
Lesbian Life and Literature
Series Editor: Karla Jay

ELIZABETH A. MEESE

(SEM)EROTICS

theorizing lesbian : writing

NEW YORK UNIVERSITY PRESS
NEW YORK AND LONDON

NEW YORK UNIVERSITY PRESS
New York and London

Library of Congress Cataloging-in-Publication Data
Meese, Elizabeth A., 1943–
(SeM) erotics: theorizing lesbian : writing / Elizabeth A. Meese.
p. cm.—(Cutting edge)
Includes bibliographical references and index.
ISBN 0-8147-5469-4—ISBN 0-8147-5470-8 (pbk.)
1. Lesbians' writings, American—History and criticism—theory, etc. 2.
American literature—Women authors—History and criticism—theory, etc. 3.
English literature—Women authors—History and criticism—theory, etc. 4.
Erotic literature—Women authors—History and criticism—Theory, etc. 5. Les-
bians' writings, English—History and criticism—Theory, etc. 6. Semiotics and
literature. 7. Feminism and literature. 8. Lesbians in literature. 9. Women and
literature. I. Title. II. Series: Cutting edge (New York, N.Y.)
PS153.L46M44 1992   92-10440
810.9'9206643—dc20   CIP

For Sandy,
who loves writing.
Yours,

The best letters of our times are precisely those that can never be published.

—Virginia Woolf, Collected Essays 2

. . . all of literature is a long letter to an invisible other, a present, a possible, or a future passion that we rid ourselves of, feed, or seek. We have also agreed that what is of interest is not so much the object of our passion, which is a mere pretext, but passion itself.

—Maria Isabel Barreno, Maria Teresa Horta, and Maria Velho da Costa, The Three Marias: New Portuguese Letters

Contents

xi

Foreword

Karla Jay

Professor of English and Women's Studies
Pace University

Despite the efforts of lesbian and feminist publishing houses
and a few university presses, the bulk of the most important
lesbian works has traditionally been available only from rare
book dealers, in a few university libraries, or in gay and lesbian
archives. This series intends, in the first place, to make representative examples of this neglected and insufficiently known
literature available to a broader audience by reissuing selected
classics and by putting into print for the first time lesbian novels,
diaries, letters, and memoirs that have special interest and significance, but which have moldered in libraries and private collections for decades or even for centuries, known only to the few
scholars who had the courage and financial wherewithal to track
them down.

Their names have been known for a long time—Sappho, the
Amazons of North Africa, the Beguines, Aphra Behn, Queen
Christina, Emily Dickinson, the Ladies of Llangollen, Radclyffe
Hall, Natalie Clifford Barney, H.D. . . . and so many others
from every nation, race, and era. But government and religious
officials burned their writings, historians and literary scholars
denied they were lesbians, powerful men kept their books out of
print, and influential archivists locked up their ideas far from
sympathetic eyes. Yet, some dedicated scholars and readers still
knew who they were, made pilgrimages to the cities and villages

xiii

where they had lived and to the graveyards where they rested. They passed around tattered volumes of letters, diaries, and biographies, in which they had underlined what seemed to be telltale hints of a secret or different kind of life. Where no hard facts existed, legends were invented. The few precious and often available pre-Stonewall lesbian classics, such as *The Well of Loneliness* by Radclyffe Hall, *The Price of Salt* by Claire Morgan [Patricia Highsmith], and *Desert of the Heart* by Jane Rule, were cherished. Lesbian pulp was devoured. One of the primary goals of this series is to give the more neglected works, which constitute the vast majority of lesbian writing, the attention they deserve.

A second but no less important aim of this series is to present the "cutting edge" of contemporary lesbian scholarship and theory across a wide range of disciplines. Practitioners of lesbian studies have not adopted a uniform approach to literary theory, history, sociology, or any other discipline, nor should they. This series intends to present an array of voices that truly reflect the diversity of the lesbian community. To help me in this task, I am lucky enough to be assisted by a distinguished editorial board that reflects various professional, class, racial, ethnic, and religious backgrounds as well as a spectrum of interests and sexual preferences.

At present lesbian studies occupies a small, precarious, and somewhat contested pied-à-terre between gay studies and women's studies. The former is still in its infancy, especially if one compares it to other disciplines that have been part of the core curriculum of every child and adolescent for several decades or even centuries. However, while one of the newest, gay studies may also be the fastest growing discipline—at least in North America. Lesbian, gay, and bisexual studies conferences are doubling or tripling their attendance. While only a handful of degree-granting programs currently exist, that number is also apt to multiply quickly in the next decade.

In comparison, women's studies is a well-established and bur-

geoning discipline with hundreds of minors, majors, and graduate programs throughout the United States. Lesbian studies
occupies a peripheral place in the curricula of such programs,
characteristically restricted to one lesbian-centered course, usually literary or historical in nature. In the many women's studies
series that are now offered by university presses, generally only
one or two books on a lesbian subject or issue are included in
each series, and lesbian voices are restricted to writing on those
topics considered of special interest to gay people. We are not
called upon to offer our opinions on motherhood, war, education, or on the lives of women not publicly identified as lesbians.
As a result, lesbian experience is too often marginalized and
restricted.

In contrast, this series will prioritize, centralize, and cele-
brate lesbian visions of literature, art, philosophy, love, religion,
ethics, history, and a myriad of other topics. In The Cutting
Edge readers can find authoritative versions of important lesbian
texts that have been carefully prepared and introduced by scholars. Readers can also find the work of academics and independent scholars who write passionately about lesbian studies and
issues or who write about other aspects of life from a distinctly
lesbian viewpoint. These visions are not only various but inten-
tionally contradictory, for lesbians speak from differing class,
racial, ethnic, and religious perspectives. Each author also speaks
from and about a certain moment of time, and few would argue
that being a lesbian today is the same as it was for Sappho or
Anne Lister. Thus, no attempt has been made to homogenize
that diversity and no agenda exists to attempt to carve out a
"politically correct" lesbian studies perspective at this juncture
in history or to pinpoint the "real" lesbians in history. It seems
more important for all the voices to be heard before those with
the blessings of aftersight lay the mantle of authenticity on any
one vision of the world, or on any particular set of women.

What each work in this series does share, however, is a
common realization that gay women are the "Other" and that
one's perception of culture and literature is filtered by sexual

behaviors and preferences. Those perceptions are not the same as those of gay men or of nongay women, whether the writers speak of gay or feminist issues or whether the writers choose to look at nongay figures from a lesbian perspective. The role of this series is to create space and give a voice to those interested in lesbian studies. This series speaks to any person who is interested in gender studies, literary criticism, biography, or important literary works, whether she or he is a student, professor, or serious reader, for it is not for lesbians only or even by lesbians only. Instead, The Cutting Edge attempts to share some of the best of lesbian literature and lesbian studies with anyone willing to look at the world through our eyes. The series is proactive in that it will help to formulate and foreground the very discipline on which it focuses. Finally, this series has answered the call to make lesbian theory, lesbian experience, lesbian lives, lesbian literature, and lesbian visions the heart and nucleus, the weighty planet around which for once other viewpoints will swirl as moons to our earth. We invite readers of all persuasions to join us by venturing into this and other books in the series.

Elizabeth Meese's *(Sem)Erotics: Theorizing Lesbian : Writing* shows the important critical trend among lesbian scholars to create or apply already existing theory to lesbian life and literature. Meese uses deconstructionist theory in a clear and readable way to bring new meaning to the lives and works of Virginia Woolf, Vita Sackville-West, Gertrude Stein, Djuna Barnes, and Nicole Brossard among others. By examining old texts with a new approach and a unique vision and by creating a dialogue about the process of doing that work, Meese asks all of us to (re)examine our relationship to the books we love, to discover whether we aren't really lovers (in every sense) of the written word when we pick up our favorite works.

Preface

In this new work, I am interested in demonstrating how a shift in institutional position, to a tenured professorship, can provide the leverage needed to pursue a different trajectory. Specifically, I want to illustrate this difference in position through another difference: the shift from the position of the writing subject I assumed in my earlier works, *Crossing the Double-Cross: The Practice of Feminist Criticism* (1986) and *(Ex)Tensions: Re-Figuring Feminist Criticism* (1990)—that of a "feminist" engaged in "writing as a 'feminist' "—to the position adopted here of a "lesbian-feminist" committed to "writing as a 'lesbian-feminist.' "

I am old enough that the politics of my position as a writing subject have been changing since I presented my dissertation, a study of American transcendentalism, in 1972—not a woman was in it. I was a lesbian when I wrote it, and a lesbian feminist when I wrote both *Crossing the Double-Cross* and *(Ex)Tensions.* This new book, *(Sem)Erotics: Theorizing Lesbian : Writing,* is markedly different in style and intent, with respect to lesbianism, than the two earlier books, and it is the only one I would claim was "written as a 'lesbian.' "

What's different about *(Sem)Erotics?* What happens besides the fact that lesbian : writing—that double-play of the "lesbian" who is writing and the "writing" that is lesbian—is taken explicitly as its subject? After all, lesbian writing (Monique Wittig in *Crossing the Double-Cross* and Adrienne Rich in *(Ex)Tensions*) has served before as my subject matter, but there is a sense in which anyone (female or male, heterosexual, homosexual, lesbian, bisexual) might have written these chapters. I want to say that politically, at least, these instances do not represent lesbian : writing for me now. This new project involves a radically other self-positioning, marked by a vivid signature, that I want to call "lesbian," and that I want readers to recognize as such.

How does it work? We could say, for example, that reading and writing as a feminist means advancing a critique of the sex-gender system, specifically the centrality of paternal authority. Who can do this work? Theoretically speaking, anyone can. We might say that the lesbian who is writing and reading as a lesbian must surrender the mask of heterosexual privilege by way of offering a critique of the ways in which lesbians are represented in discursive fields.

The distinction I want to make—between the lesbian (who is) writing and the lesbian (who is) "writing as a lesbian"—is one between "writing about" and "writing with (or as)" one's subject; that is, how one takes one's "place" in language. In *(Sem)Erotics*, I am interested in exploring textual erotics beyond content, acknowledging the blurred boundaries between the personal and the critical, the particular, concrete intimacy of sexual expression, and the (for some) abstract aridity of high theory. I am self-consciously the subject of/in writing, placing my lesbian : writing alongside that of my subjects—Woolf, Stein, Barnes, Brossard and others. Our texts, like sexual bodies, are intercalated, interpolated, one engaged with and added to another.

Acknowledgments

My gratitude to Claudia Johnson continues, unflagging, as she is in her affection. For support and advice, I thank my friends at home: Harold Weber, Francesca Kazan, Sharon O'Dair, Carol Pierman, Alice Parker, Jean Mills and Carol Eichelberger. For the inspiration of courageous work, I thank Nicole Brossard. For the dailiness of her encouragement and assistance, Sandy Huss, and for their persistence of vision and effort, Karla Jay and Joanne Glasgow.

Responsive audiences at the University of Calgary (thanks to Eric Savoy), the University of Edmonton (thanks to Janice Williamson), and OUT/WRITE 1991 (thanks to Kevin Killian) made my project easier, as did Niko Pfund and the staff of New York University Press.

English graduate students—Michelle Hippler, Ann Coyle, Kathy Day and Ellen Gandt—made substantial contributions to my research efforts. I am further grateful to the University of Alabama Research Grants Committee, which provided summer grant support in 1989 so that I could complete chapters 2 and 5.

Chapter 1 appeared in a slightly different version in *Lesbian Texts and Contexts: Radical Revisions*, edited by Karla Jay and Joanne Glasgow. A version of chapter 2 appeared in *Feminist Studies* 18 (1992). An excerpt from the book appeared in the *South Atlantic Review* (May 1992).

Grateful acknowledgment is made for permission to reprint the following material:

Daphne Marlatt and Nicole Brossard, *Character/Jeu de Lettres* (copyright © 1986, by Daphne Marlatt and Nicole Brossard and nbj) by permission of the authors; Nicole Brossard, *Sous La*

Langue/Under Tongue, trans. Susanne de Lotbinière-Harwood. Copyright Brossard; Lotbinière-Harwood and Gynergy Books, 1987. Used by permission of Gynergy Books; Nicole Brossard, *Lovhers*, trans. Barbara Godard, copyright Brossard; Godard and Guernica, 1986. Used by permission of Guernica Editions; Becky Birtha's "Plumstone" from *By Word of Mouth*, ed. Lee Fleming; Reprinted with permission of Gynergy Books. Copyright Lee Fleming, 1989; Excerpt from *Beginning with O* reprinted with permission of the author and of Yale University Press. Copyright Olga Broumas, 1977; Excerpt from *Perpetua* reprinted with permission of Copper Canyon Press. Copyright Olga Broumas, 1989; Letter excerpt reprinted with the permission of Jon-Henri Damski; Gertrude Stein, "Lifting Belly" and "Idem the Same" reprinted with the permission of the Estate of Gertrude Stein, and also for *Lifting Belly*, reprinted with permission of Naiad Press. Copyright Rebecca Mark, 1989; "Ramon" by Laurie Anderson © 1989 Difficult Music (BMI); Cover photograph by Gay Burke, to whom I extend thanks as always for being the photographer and generous friend that she is.

ONE

Theorizing Lesbian : Writing—
A Love Letter

. . . reality begins with the intention of you
—Nicole Brossard, *Lovhers*

It is always a matter of waking up, but never of some first awakening. My own presence to myself has been preceded by a language. Older than consciousness, older than the spectator, prior to any attendance, a sentence awaits "you": looks at you, observes you, watches over you, and regards you from every side. There is always a sentence that has already been sealed somewhere waiting for you where you think you are opening up some virgin territory.
—Jacques Derrida, *Dissemination*

Analysis is a womanly word. It means that they discover there are laws.
—Gertrude Stein, *How to Write*

Why is it that the lesbian seems like a shadow—a shadow with/in woman, with/in writing? A contrastive shape in a shadow play, slightly formless, the edges blurred by the turns of the field, the sheets on which a drama is projected. The lesbian subject is not all I am and it is in all I am. A shadow of who I am that attests to my being there, I am never with/out this lesbian. And we are always turning, this way and that, in one place and another. The shadows alone, never mind the body, make such a complex choreography in the contest with sense. An architectonics of light and shade, moving, converging and I have only begun to describe the body in its shadow state, in two dimensions, in the equally shadowy medium of words. What could be the auto-bio-graph-y of this figure, of this writing "lesbian"? The word, the letter "L" and the lesbian of this auto-biography, this auto-graph? I like the letter "L" which contains its own shadow, makes and is made up of shadow, so that I cannot de-cipher the thing from its reflection. Does the horizontal stroke throw itself upward? Or is it the vertical stroke which casts its long shadow on the ground? The question of which is thing and what is shadow depends upon where I stand, or how I regard the letter. And is it the case that the body is always more substantial than the shadow it casts? I used to think so, but now this question appears familiar, like the old conundrums of figure and ground, content and form, body and mind. How then to begin to say what lesbian : writing is, to write its story, to speak of the letter of the letter?

In "Zero Degree Deviancy" Catharine R. Stimpson defines "the lesbian" in a "conservative and severely literal" way: "She is a woman who finds other women erotically attractive and gratifying" (364). Her definition, she says, holds to the "literal," or we might say, the "letteral"—to the body, which seems like the lesbian body, or perhaps to the word as the em-bodied inscription of lesbian : writing: "That carnality distinguishes it from gestures of political sympathy with homosexuals and from affectionate friendships in which women enjoy each other, support each other, and commingle a sense of identity, and well-being. Lesbianism represents a commitment of skin, blood, breast, and bone" (364). But the literal body, however powerfully evoked, is a referential one, the "skin" and "bone" of textuality's absent lesbian, "there," and, literally speaking, not there at all, whose "being" depends on the word's evocation. She is called forth, in the way that I see your figure on the page, make you present for me as I write my letter to you. Your body is only as "literal" as the letter, the shade and angle of the marks on a page, the course of associations or forms in the mind, an/other instance of some mysterious relation between the word and the flesh. What, then, does it mean to claim, as Stimpson does, that lesbian writing springs from some other "physical presence in the world" (364)?

Writing the lesbian means writing someone who does not yet exist. This is not a project I take lightly, for as Nicole Brossard reminds us, "A lesbian who does not reinvent the word is a lesbian in the process of disappearing" (*Aerial* 122). Writing demands that I bring a "self" (I could say "myself") into existence. A self I create as I write, as I say "I" and "lesbian," searching for the words, syntax and grammar that can articulate the body, my body, and perhaps yours. When I write my love letter to you, I want to bring myself to you, hand myself over. When I write about lesbian : writing, I take my life in my hands, as my text. Or is it that I take my text as my life in my search for a language capable of expressing what those words—lesbian : writing—mean when our fingers, soft and electric, just meet, pulled together by their own magnetically charged engagement as (though) they have a life, a movement, of their own. Or when my tongue slides over the osmotic, lively breathing surfaces of your skin like words in the more elusive *glissement*, gliding like waves, one just over the other, enveloping their letters, as, in their representational capacity, they produce signification which we take as meanings. Or as the pen makes its tracks across the body of the page, its friction and its struggle to mark the course faithfully, our passions inscribed energetically in the body of language in the mind: a love letter.

The Letter of the Law

Lesbian : writing takes (its) place in a semantic field subject to, that is, ordering itself and us, around the phallus (the prick of the phallo-logo-centric system). According to its rule, all subjects are subject to the law of the phallus if we are to found ourselves as speakers, in other words, to (pro)claim an identity. Luce Irigaray suggests in this respect that "we might suspect the phallus (Phallus) of being the *contemporary figure of a god jealous of his prerogatives;* we might suspect it of claiming, on this basis, to be the ultimate meaning of all discourse, the standard of truth and propriety, in particular as regards sex, the signifier and/or the ultimate signified of all desire, in addition to continuing, as emblem and agent of the patriarchal system, to shore up the name of the father (Father)" (*This Sex* 67). This phallic reign, in the interest of perpetuating and replicating itself, writes itself as the law of representation and representationality. But the law hides itself, a condition, we might suspect, of its effectiveness. This is what Lacan means when he says that the phallus "can play its role only when veiled" (*Écrits* 288).

The law—like reason, its regulatory agent—drives a system, polices it, while pretending that it is not itself written in it. It refuses to appear, representing itself as being above the law. Derrida offers a variation on this theme in "Sending": "Perhaps law itself outreaches any representation, perhaps it is never before us, as what posits itself in a figure or composes a figure for itself" (325). We read the effects of the Law but never the Law-itself. (The problem again of the "L"—what is substance, what is shadow?) By hiding, the Law escapes revision and protects its autocratic rule. As speaking subjects, we are positioned before it. Thus, Derrida observes in the terms of Kafka's parable, "The guardian of the law and the man from the country are 'before the law,' *Vor dem Gesetz*, says Kafka's title, only at the cost of never coming to see it, never being able to arrive at it. It is neither presentable nor representable, and the 'entry' into it, according to an order which the man from the country interiorizes and gives himself, is put off until death" ("Sending" 325). Such is the subject's double-bind: were we to arrive "there," we would no longer be "before" the law, that is, subject to it. It saves itself, perpetuates our subjugation, by its refusal to (re)present itself to us, to show its face, to allow itself to be seen, except through its effects, which we frequently apprehend with difficulty and (mis)take for the Law-itself. We read it as we read a dream which writes us and is written by us. Brossard describes its operation and effects as follows: "as soon as we speak of culture, we necessarily speak of codes, signs, exchanges, communication, and recognition. Likewise, we must speak of a system of values which, on the one hand, determines what makes sense or non-sense and which, on the other, normalizes sense so that eccentricity, marginality, and transgression can be readily identified as such, in order to control them if need be" (*Aerial* 103). In language, as we take on "selves" by speaking our positions, we offer ourselves up for regulation. The sentence awaits us. The paradoxical condition of being "before," which we have accepted in order to speak, remains in effect/affect until death.

The issue here for the feminist and lesbian reader/writer is to consider what it means to be "there" (even if "there" is "nowhere"), like it or not, standing before the Law as that which regulates "the acquisition of an interpretive fiction" we call knowledge (Causse, "L'Interloquée" 79). Our task is to discover ways to challenge and to subvert the Law before death, to risk it through unthinkable (non-sensical) forms of resistance. What, after all, do I have to lose by breaking the Law? There is a special sense in which Derrida's comments concerning the Law's refusal to be represented pertains to woman; that is, we have a particular stake in its application. He writes, "The law has often been considered as that which puts things in place, posits itself and gathers itself up in composition (thesis, *Gesetz*, in other words what governs the order of representation), and autonomy in this respect always presupposes representation, as thematization, becoming-theme" ("Sending" 325–26). Does woman, as she author-izes her "own" discourse, represent herself as "herself," or is she merely an effect of the Law at work? What Law operates at the borderline of life and text in her work of "self"-composition? Can she, in Michèle Causse's words, set up some woman-ordered regulative technology (gynolect) and/or take over his language ("androlect," an idiolect masquerading as the only "sexolect") and, with it, his "place" ("L'Interloquée" 80–82)?

Causse responds to these questions by proposing a shocking, scandalous shift in the sex/gender system (sexualization, she points out elsewhere, "plays like segregation" ["Le monde" 14]) which involves the rewriting of man (presumably defined, like woman, by "conceptual capacities" rather than "biological properties" ["L'Interloquée" 88]) as sole occupant of the subject position and his relegation to the place of "second" person (the [no]"place" of the second sex?)—"hey, *you* (over) there." As Causse puts it, the "adress(h)er" "creates the scandal of a male 'we' shifted onto the site of the 'you' " ("L'Interloquée" 86–87). Having achieved a reversal, Causse presses for a heterogeneity in which "be-ing" (not "man," who was always speaking, nor "woman," who was always silent) takes up the subject position. Causse's strategy achieves a startling effect rather like the deconstructive reversal where relations of power are exchanged, as she moves us toward the ultimately desired displacement which might trans-form the structure of relations. The reversal without displacement can only be satisfying for the lesbian whose *personal* stake/investment rests in the domination of men, and not particularly in the liberation of "women" and "men." This poses problems of definition—who is that man and this woman/lesbian?—and of solidarity with "brothers," who, like homosexual and third world men, may have more (and less) ambiguous relations to phallic authority and masculine privilege.

What if I want to address, as I do now, a beautiful woman—you about us, you and me? When, in my letter, I write *I love you* what am I writing? Who am "I" then, and who are "you"? (Isn't this always our problem?)

Both Causse and Wittig locate the preliminary work of a revolution in lesbian : writing in the subject of writing, as writing: *Je* (Causse, "Le monde" 15). It is as though, through a properly improper writing, the contract with the father's Law, which constitutes the female (subject) as object, can be shattered. The letters composing the subject are broken apart: j/e. Wittig describes the radical violence of lesbian : writing when she says, in her prefatory note to *The Lesbian Body*, " 'I' *[Je]* as a generic feminine subject can *only* enter by force into a language which is foreign to it, for all that is human (masculine) is foreign to it, the human not being feminine grammatically speaking but he *[il]* or they *[ils]*. . . . 'I' *[Je]* obliterates the fact that *elle* or *elles* are submerged in *il* or *ils*, i.e., that all the feminine persons are complementary to the masculine persons" (10). This is the condition of woman writing who "cannot be 'un écrivain' " (10). We do not dare forget that, as Irigaray puts it in *Speculum of the Other Woman*, "any theory of the 'subject' has always been appropriated by the 'masculine' " (133). Thus Wittig inscribes her alienation and resistance in the body of the word: "*J/e* is the symbol of the lived, rending experience which is m/y writing, of this cutting in two which throughout literature is the exercise of a language which does not constitute m/e as subject. *J/e* poses the ideological and historic question of feminine subjects" (10–11). A mutilation of the word that slashes the subject's presumptive unicity, J/e, like the mark of the hysterical symptom, stands (in) as the inscription of violence on the body of the (female) subject. Lesbian : writing, in this sense, turns on the Father as phallus, the big prick who regulates the construction of woman. It turns him into the figure that he is—a linguistic site in which substitutions can occur, a rhetorical trope which is subject to revision and re-motivation in a re-writing where woman attempts "the conquest of an *I [Je]*" (Causse, "Le monde" 15).

Unlike the symptom, the body's inscription of its unconscious conflict with itself or the world, this broken sign, j/e, marks a certain willful triumph. It signals a response to the problem of acquiring lesbianism as my sign, how to take it on as part of me: I-lesbian, the sign that stands for me when I say "I." Language, the letter, stands in for me when I am away, not there. I can only enter language as a subject by speaking myself. I construct myself, make myself a lesbian subject, by giving myself a sign, which also means a signification and a value, and by addressing myself to a woman I want to (be) like me. The subject is the "first" person, not the second (the problem we always have as we love each other), and certainly not the third, the object or "thing" spoken of. This j/e that I take on says, "look at me, look what you have made of me, look at what I must now do to (re)present myself."

The Law of the Letter

To write lesbianism is to enter a rhetorical, that is, a meta-phorical, field—a scene of "transposition . . . [involving] the *figure as such*" and a scene of "*resemblance*" (Ricoeur 17). In other words, when I write (of) the lesbian, I engage the problem of speaking metaphorically about metaphor, or representation-ally of representation. Through resemblances, I write "in other words" of the "woman" and her "lesbian"/shadow, or the "les-bian" and her "woman"/shadow, of "me" and "you." Metaphor speaks a language of deviation, the quality of something at-tributed to something else (its transposition), as well as meaning both anchored (materialized in the figure) and adrift (transferring from figure to figure) from some always unknown origin. Ricoeur explains that metaphor as a "categorical transgression" can be "understood as a deviation in relation to a pre-existing logical order, as a dis-ordering in a scheme of classification. This transgression is interesting only because it creates meaning . . . should we not say that metaphor destroys an order only to invent a new one; and that the category-mistake is nothing but the complement of a logic of discovery?" (Ricoeur 22). In addition, the order destroyed or supplanted by metaphor is itself an/other metaphorical representation. Lesbian : writing creates a curious case where the metaphoric language of deviation (of substitution, drift and trans-position) is put in the service of writing what culture has historically regarded as deviation (as aberration and perversion). Claudie Lesselier puts this in slightly different terms when she describes the tension inhabiting the lesbian subject as both included in and standing against the social discourse which produces it, the effect of the letter of the law in tension with the law of the letter. The lesbian subject exhibits a "tension be-tween, on the one hand, *claiming a category* (by giving it an-other meaning) and, on the other hand, *subverting the whole system of categorization*" (93). Creation/destruction. It is pre-cisely this project of subversion as aberration and as trans-position which preoccupies lesbian : writing.

Lesbian theorizing is always at once theoretical and "pre"-theoretical: the writer behaves as though she knows what the lesbian is, what theorizing lesbianism entails, despite what Mary Daly and Jane Caputi term its "wildness," what is "not accounted for by any known theories" (100). The "pre"-theoretical of lesbian theorizing is and is not a "pre"- on its way to becoming something in itself, is and is not a stage of anticipation before the letter—a "pre"- waiting to be "post"-. The lesbian writer presents her subject as (the) One in the absence of others. Her lesbian, the lesbian in her, is made "present" in language, standing as representative for and representation of the one(s) not here. Her words contend with the polysemy and polyvocality of an unlimited field, striking (down) limits with every word she writes in a signifying system which prefers dimorphic binarism to polymorphic abundance, feigning presence when every word stands in for some one or some thing else/where. "L." It cannot be denied that there is something of *capital* importance here, a capital investment in/of the letter—a remainder, a sentence, a matter of principle importance, counting on a return.

When I write *I love you,* I act as though I know who I am and what it means to love. And who you are, and that you will understand what it means to me to tell you. I have to write as though we are together in this.

If language/text, in its metaphorical activity, always comes back to itself, defers and refers to itself in uncanny ways, what keeps woman within the system of its control when its ability to control and to regulate is already failed, incomplete, deficient? As such, one law of language—definition/signification (the need for woman as the "other" of the symbolic system) is at odds with another—language's inability to control and to determine itself perfectly or completely: (the lesbian slips in). She will always escape, slide in and/or out through the bar(s), and, like it or not, so will some of her fugitive and rebellious sisters and brothers. In her description of the slippery imperfection of language, Brossard suggests how this might occur: "It doesn't take much for *god* to become *dog,* and it takes nothing, in French, for 'she is named' [Elle est comme on nomme] to be heard as 'she is like a man' [Elle est comme un homme]. The magic of words is also this way with which, and this 'what' with which we can transform reality or the sense we give it" (*Aerial* 107). In the gaps, the "holes" or the "spaces," by a willful (though erratic/erotic) trajectory, comes desire, excess. Woman comes. I could say, then, that our tasks involve learning to be an "escape artist," and making an art, by perfecting our techniques, of such a criminal behavior. The love letter is a secret letter, making its way out.

The need for these trans-formative arts grows apparent as we begin to write. Almost with the first word, we encounter the Rule of contemporary theorizing: it is forbidden "to essentialize" woman or lesbian, to claim an essence, a nature or some particular properties for woman as woman-in-herself. On balance (what the rule is about), this is not a bad proscription since such a speaking of woman-as-woman and lesbian-as-lesbian has resulted in the problems we contend with now. In a sense, we are always, after our detours, returning to it, can't help but return to this place even when we think we are discussing the way in which the social text writes woman-as-woman. There is a sense in which phallocentrism, heterosexism, feminism and lesbianism (homosexuality as well) are, paradoxically, effects of the Law of the Same. As Derrida suggests to Christie McDonald, "phallocentrism and homosexuality can go, so to speak, hand in hand, and I take these terms, whether it is a question of feminine or masculine homosexuality, in a very broad and radical sense" ("Choreographies" 72). Surely, we want to say, this odd coupling, phallocentrism and lesbianism, shows the phallocratic philosopher for what he is. But this is the very trap Wittig and others seek to escape by positioning the word "lesbian" outside of the sex-gender con/figuration, outside the opposition man/woman and heterosexual/homosexual, the terms of which present themselves to us, have their differences founded, in just these essential ways (Wittig, "Mark" 7–11; "Paradigm" 118–21).

Nonetheless, we must admit that there is a certain terror in the notion of sexuality set out by Derrida and, in another way, by Wittig and Felix Guattari and Gilles Deleuze: Gone "the woman." Unlike Derrida, Wittig has a personal, political and theoretical investment in wanting to claim something special for the lesbian as not-"woman," not-"man." But what can lesbianism be without "woman" as sex or gender? Man/woman: lesbian. Wittig wants to make "lesbian" an/other "place"—the site of a gap, a space or a rupture in the oppositional rule-driven system of signification. Outlaw that she is, Wittig wants to position the lesbian "outside the Law." She maintains, "The designation 'woman' will disappear no doubt just as the designation 'man' with the oppression/exploitation of women as a class by men as a class. Humankind must find another name for itself and another system of grammar that will do away with genders, the linguistic indicator of political oppression" ("Paradigm" 121). A threat declares itself in multiple, polymorphous sexuality, where there is difference but not the two: beyond man/woman. Derrida offers us an/other representation: "a chorus, for a choreographic text with polysexual signatures" which "goes beyond known or coded marks, beyond the grammar and spelling, shall we say (metaphorically) of sexuality." Finally, he arrives at the most provocative question: "what if we were to approach here (for one does not arrive at this as one would at a determined location) the area of a relationship to the other where the code of sexual marks would no longer be discriminating? The relationship would not be a-sexual, far from it, but would be sexual otherwise: beyond the binary difference that governs the decorum of all codes, beyond the opposition feminine/ masculine, beyond bi-sexuality as well, beyond homosexuality and heterosexuality which come to the same thing" ("Choreographies" 76).

What is this "sexual otherwise," the "beyond" of sexuality, "beyond" lesbianism, as we name them today? The elaboration Derrida offers elsewhere is richly suggestive: "At that point there would be no more sexes . . . there would be one sex for each time. One sex for each gift. A sexual difference for each gift. That can be produced within the situation of a man and a woman, a man and a man, a woman and a woman, three men and a woman, etc. By definition, one cannot calculate the gift. We are in the order of the incalculable, of undecidability which is a strategic undecidability where one says 'it is undecidable because it is not this term of the opposition or the other.' This is sexual difference. It is absolutely heterogeneous" ("Women" 199). Similarly, Wittig notes that "For us there are, it seems, not one or two sexes but many (cf. Guattari/Deleuze), as many sexes as there are individuals" ("Paradigm" 119). This is the step away from "the true sex" constructed in the inte₁est of guaranteeing heterosexuality/reproduction. The play of sexes recalls Christiane Rochefort's discovery through writing that she also had homosexual fantasies: "I didn't have them 'consciously,' but it was something in me nonetheless. . . . But something that, all things considered, I would have liked. Had I been a man I would have been homosexual too. Both. Another triumph. Be all four sexes. All four. Yes" (112–13). She counts to four, the easy multiplication of male/female, homosexual/heterosexual. Another reckoning, one of a "lesbian" abundance, might yield up more. Where, then, in this wide field of play, this wildness of heterogeneous sexual difference and of theorizing, is the "woman," the "lesbian" and "lesbianism"? What does it mean to insist, as Brossard repeatedly does, "To write *I am a woman* is full of consequence" ["Écrire *je suis une femme* est plein de conséquences"] (*L'Amer* 53)? What's in the name?[1]

Because we do not know, or in order to know, we answer anyway. We write, just as I am writing my love letter to you, in the belief that we can say something theoretical or philosophical (or personal and intimate) about "lesbianism," *as if* "experience" and "self-definition," in opposition to philosophical argument, were distinct from metaphoric turns. We might even say that writing compels us to behave this way. Or at least we write out of a belief in the value of seeking an answer. We write (or want to, can't help but write) as though lesbianism were an already there of/in the real, a direct ontology, because "language," as Wittig points out, "casts sheaves of reality upon the social body, stamping it and violently shaping it" ("Mark" 4). What is it, after all, to be a (lesbian) without the word, without writing *l-e-s-b-i-a-n* or something like it? It seems like nothing. So I write, and in doing so, I enter metaphor, or metaphor enters me. I take up my grammatical place: the lesbian subject. Though it seems to provide a ready-made structure, metaphor allows the writer to defy the tidy organization of container and contained. In this regard, Hélène Cixous explains how figures dislocate language: "metaphor breaks free; all that belongs to the realm of fantasmatic production (*la production fantasmatique*), all that belongs to the imaginary and smashes language from all sides represents a force that cannot be controlled. Metaphors are what drive language mad" (71). Like description, figuration works on the principle of likeness, resemblances of one thing to another ("the lesbian is . . ."; "lesbianism is . . ."). Slippages enter even as this writing wants to answer what it is we want and even need to know. "L." Additionally, or further, in the resemblance of one thing to another, there is always an absence. Absence is "further" (beyond); absence is "added" to what the figure stands for. There is resemblance but not identity—likeness to the thing but never the thing itself or the thing-in-itself ("The mimeme is neither the thing itself nor something totally other," Derrida, *Margins* 240 fn 43). So that at the heart of the very description which is supposed to give us lesbian presence, lesbian identity, this absence lingers. You and I, as lesbian women, are not there in the sentence. As works like Daly's *Gyn/Ecology* and Daly and Caputi's dictionary suggest, lesbians often speak as though we can re-invent language to write a new identity, to make us present.

It may be more appropriate to say that lesbian : writing wants to evacuate patriarchal discourse in order to re-write writing. The vacancy, the absence on/in which I dwell, (re)presents the space for writing which writers like Brossard want to create, the break in the semiotic surface the lesbian/woman slips through: "Unconsciously, and for all time, the knowing body opposes itself to the learned letter. But everybody knows, what counts is the letter. I write in self-defense. If I can find the lost stream, writing interests me" (*Aerial* 39–40). The lesbian writer seeks to intervene in language, reinvent, or better, re-work its texture, to produce an exploratory language through which we can find ourselves as subject and (of) desire.

Dear "L,"

I miss you. I've been working very hard on the first chapter of my book. There's always a rush at the start of a new project, like the point where a runner glides into overdrive (I've been watching the Olympics too). It's reassuring to know that I'm not finished. But this project is the best one yet because, when I write about lesbianism, it is easy to imagine that I am writing to you. We are together on the page. Sometimes I hear you saying the words just ahead of me, as if you were writing me writing.

And that word, "lesbian." Can you tell me whose word it is? When, and under what circumstances, did you first hear it? Or did you initially read it on a page somewhere, since it more often goes unspoken? Does it come from "within" or from "without"? It is a double word (play): the turn of the tongue on the letter tells me what it means, whether one way or the other. "Lesbian" is applied to me in a system I do not control, that cannot control itself. Yet it is a word I want to embrace, re-write and re-claim, not to install it but to explode its meaning in the shuttle motion from the pejorative (mis)understandings of the "outside" of lesbianism to what I want to create as an energetics, a (sem)erotics, an affectionate designation of the "inside" lesbianism. How we speak of it to one another. Through the dynamic interaction I present the site of the word, a "beyond" lesbianism that is neither the fixed place of the damned nor the (ec)static transcendental position of the saved—those polarities Stimpson calls "the dying fall, a narrative of damnation" and the "enabling escape, a narrative of reversal" (364). Language is not "outside" me, except in the way that skin is "outside" the body. No skin, no body. The body is already in(side) language. Lesbian is the word/name a given woman chooses for her idea of herself, to represent her idea (representation) of herself. I am/you are/she is/we are that place where wor(l)ds of meaning collide.

It is hard for me to believe that the question of "lesbian being" should be exempt from the Derridean critique of being in general (*Grammatology*, chap. 1)—something we presume and assume, attributing to it some essential or transcendental status, in order to speak about it. In their varied and powerful ways, lesbian women of color have been cautioning white feminists from the beginning; Barbara Smith, Gloria Anzaldua, Audre Lorde, among the many women who (re)mark the color of the letter "L": Lorde describes the false pretense to "homogeneity of experience covered by the word *sisterhood*" (*Sister* 116); Smith wants to discover, when reading, a letter addressed to her and the black women she loves (183–84); and Anzaldua performs the beautiful complexity of her *mestiza* heritage in the linguistic shifts and slides on the pages of *Borderlands;/La Frontera.* Caution all around.

So it is both before and after the letter, before and after what I write about it. How else could I ever say *I love you?* "Lesbian being" is something which is "there," when "there" shifts and ex-changes itself to suit the speaker, who also ex-changes herself (making more of us). The critiques of identity and presence suggest that we "leave open the question of this energetic absence" (Derrida, *Margins* 240), the means by which I am always describing lesbianism. Thus, I am always writing, describing "the lesbian" as an il-licit (unreadable, *illisible*, or unwritable) woman, whose meaning I am constantly called upon to (re)produce:

> she has no character meaning
> indissoluble boundaries
> s/he:
> s plural in excess of he
> (Marlatt and Brossard)

What can be said about this difference in the letter: the *s/* of *s/ he?* What difference does (the) difference make? The supplement of excess. Why is it an extra, a difference, in the first place? The extra, extrinsic quality is precisely the problem: the problem of "firstness," of the first place.

I would like to think that lesbianism, like feminism, could position itself "outside." There's a comfort in the tidiness offered by the absence of complicity and the certainty of an absolute difference. But lesbianism, as an attack on hetero-relations, takes (its) place within the structure of the institution of heterosexuality. The lesbian is born of/in it. We know the condition(ing) is not fatal, just as we mark its torturous limits. It might even afford a strategic value to be "there," if Derrida is right that attacks occur from within, because attacks "are not possible and effective, nor can they take accurate aim, except by inhabiting those structures. Inhabiting them *in a certain way*, because one always inhabits, and all the more when one does not suspect it." But, as Derrida continues, danger lurks in this structural relation: "Operating necessarily from the inside, borrowing all the strategic and economic resources of subversion from the old structure, borrowing them structurally . . . the enterprise of deconstruction always in a certain way falls prey to its own work" (*Grammatology* 24). The illusionary and visionary project (it must be both of these) of lesbianism is to be writing the "beyond" of heterosexual phallogocentrism, even though this is also what is always recuperating us, claiming to (re)produce us as one of its effects. I am in writing and writing is in me. I am no different from what I say about it, no better, no worse. When I speak of its structures, I speak of myself, even in resistance. Language over/takes me, and I am over/come. I say again and again *I love you*.

Some kind of terror disguises itself when an excess is pronounced, like the terror of Derrida's speculation on sex, his "no" to lesbianism and feminism. Because it goes "beyond" us, we do not know what "it" is in this unsettling economy of excess. The step beyond. Step, no step, two step; Derrida's *pas de thèse* (*Post Card* 293) leaves me without a position, a place that I can

count on, or on the basis of which I can calculate the risks and
the gains. A specter presents itself in the fear of speculation.
Yes, this shadow asks for identification, differentiation. Is it me?
Or not me, but you? Is it there at all, an effect of speculation's
own fear? What path can lead us to the "yes" of the "lesbian"
beyond the male-female opposition of hetero-relational feminism
(Raymond 4), "the lesbian" beyond the Derridean refusal of
lesbianism as homosexuality's opposition to heterosexuality (terms
he also refuses)?

When you look at me, what do you see? I try to read the signs
of it in your eyes. On the street, I see only the women, and
more, when I look at a particular woman, I see only the les-
bian(s) in her, the woman to whom I want to address my letter,
the pleasure we could have together. When I look at you, I
never want to see myself without you or in any other way. I want
to see the woman/lesbian you are and what you see in me. None
of this is easy. It requires an effort of mind for which there are
no certain signs or protocols.

In lesbianism we exchange our bodies and their properties in
an economy where woman places woman (herself) in circulation.
Lesbianism installs an un-utterable difference of difference—
"I"/"me" and "my lover," "she"/"me"—in the woman, as a double woman, a double subject: "she" and "she." It provides for
the breaking open of the phallocratically constructed "woman,"
passed from hand to hand, always a "woman" who knows herself
only as a "man's woman" in a series of "hetero"sexual contracts.
The lesbian goes and comes, a departure and a return. Hers is a
profitable absence, produces "more" writing, the undecidability
of which permits, indeed requires, us to produce other writings,
other likenesses, diversity, change. My not-knowing produces
this speculation, and in the interest of future speculation, something in me does not want to know. In/completion motivates our
compulsion, our obsession, and, better still, our passion for the
return, the repetition as reappearance of the lesbian-in-writing,
who, in coming *again*, comes a second and a third time as though

recalling that illusory, shadowy first time, and, of course, the first (mythically originary) Lesbian—the narrative of her appearance before. In telling this story, I come again and again. How will you kr. ɔw if I am a c(o)unterfeit or the "real" thing, if "it" is really happening, if this letter is authentic or a forgery? Whether or not it is really you and I and love that I mean when I write *I love you?*

"Lesbian" is a word written in invisible ink, readable when held up to a flame and self-consuming, a disappearing trick before my eyes where the letters appear and fade into the paper on which they are written, like a field which inscribes them. An unwriting goes on as quickly as the inscription takes (its) place. Not the erasure of time's vast conspiratorial silence, that invisibility censoriously imposed on us, but an un-writing as carefully prepared and enacted as the act of lesbian : composition itself. Lesbian. This word which, like us, threatens to disappear is one we must demand, say over and over again, re-calling it. Lesbian, les-bian, -bian, *bien*, "L," *lesbienne:* a word that won't stay put. Adrienne Rich discusses the stakes we understand so well: "The word lesbian must be affirmed because to discard it is to collaborate with silence and lying about our very existence; with the closet-game, the creation of the *unspeakable*" (*On Lies* 202). In the interest of staging a resistance, I want to re-write writing, write (it) over again, returning, coming again.

I want this word to be a place where my story is not known to myself, to anyone; where the story of the other remains also a mystery, always being solved or written—made and unmade every day like Penelope's handwork. A place between the ecstasy of desire and passion, and of arrest, silence, not knowing. A space where both occur. The danger of love always inhabits the other. The bar, lesbian life, the bedroom where passion is found and made, but also dangerous places of discovery, exchange, and loss. "There is," Brossard writes, "consistency in wanting all orgasmic bliss clandestine even though it might happen openly" (*These* 76). The passion is not in the repetition of a pattern, a way, but in a going (off), in anticipation and confrontation with the danger and/in the prospect. The pattern wants to enforce itself, imprint itself beyond interrogation, beyond the energizing forces of not knowing, discovering and creating. Against arrest which is more *(arrêt)* than it seems. I am still amazed by the way the smallest stroke can occasion an extraordinary moment of surprise.

Some encounters mark a turning point. Picking up the book, a love gift, I turn away from solitary speculation into the course of words, articulations of pleasure that ask for a response. The pleasure in/of writing as engagement stands in for other pleasures—a kiss or an embrace; perhaps just a touch. Not the thing itself, which a photo might pretend to show, but the feeling or fusion of passion in a few simple strokes which might always only, even by choice or circumstance, remain in the regard—the glance, the slight correction or connection of the eyes with a letter on the page. So when her lover is no longer or not ever there, the writer returns to writing, the engagement I can produce when the lover and my love for her are nothing other than but are at least no less than a memory.

I approach the white body of the page—stroke its surface as I would your skin—inscribing on it what I take as literal signs of my affection, sometimes with an animated passion, sometimes with a thoughtfully gentle contemplation.[2] Surface to surface which, like all inscriptions, connect beyond to some deeper, more powerful significances. Something happens as well in the mind where love is an inventive gesture.

After writing, after reading, we no longer make love the same way. The words are no longer ours, as we (re)write how "Chloe loved Olivia" but not for the first time in English letters; certainly not only in English, and perhaps beyond the letter. We cannot make love alone. The other lesbian, the writer-lover, produces our amazement at how words, joy and play, passion come together; the body, the memory, the language of the writer compel us in a synergystic field of circulating energies, but without the closure such a systemic metaphor suggests. Instead, there is incompletion where energy jumps the synapses, from the word of one to the word of another, from one tongue to another, experiences translated, language transmuting in an engagement with the word as hot as when the writer and her electric lover-reader meet, as though when the hands touch, or when the finger turns the page, passion sparks. Ignition. Trans-literation.

No, we are far from alone. There are three or four, maybe five of us, the other('s) words encircling kaleidoscopically—"conch-shell" and "coral," "the seacarved pip" (Causse, *Lesbiana* 25–26), "the little pearl" (Brossard, *Sous la langue*), the "little scallop" in its moist, warm bed, the "peony" and the "winter pear" (Lorde, *Zami* 139). Others participate as I consider "that small rose-coloured anemone dredged from the depths of the sea opening out under my exploring fingers. A moon-like spectre emerged from that innocent sea-flower and made my heart throb" (Maraini 35). Leaf after leaf, an explosive f(r)iction as one lover, then the next or several, five works together, go off—an explosion in the seme (seem). At this moment, it is easier to think of the body than the letter, its pulsations—regular and then not so regular. It is more difficult to say what this f(r)iction means to the delicate anemone, the sea flower whose tendrils g(r)asp and a-spire toward orgasm, the f(r)iction of the pen, of the letter in a revolutionary play becoming lesbian : writing in a spark(l)ing, glistening chain. One word always in the company of another and another. Did we find these words or did they find us? Did the "real" scene write the text or did the text compose the scene? The words of love multiply, acquire color and form, powerful descriptions, yes even determinants, of what we are doing in our lesbian silence. This is what I mean when I say that the lesbian-writer (re)writes us as "ourselves." Words are never alone. But for me, reading and writing are not enough. Without you, or at least my narrative memory of you, after the page has been signed, with just me and these words, mine and/or yours, hers, theirs, I recall how the ecstasy of the letter—once

the continual acts of re-memorization and reinfusion wane—
eventually fades.

> Looking for you,
> Love,
> "L"

P.S. Sorry about my wandering, unruly letter. Try to wait up for
me. I'll return by evening on Friday; perhaps I'll even come
before my letter.

TWO

When Virginia Looked at Vita, What Did She See; or,
Lesbian : Feminist : Woman—What's the Differ(e/a)nce?

I am reduced to a thing that wants Virginia.
> —Vita Sackville-West, *Letters of
> Vita Sackville-West to Virginia Woolf*

I lie in bed making up stories about you.
> —Virginia Woolf to Vita Sackville-West

"I don't know if love's a feeling. Sometimes I think it's a matter of seeing. Seeing you."
> —Marguerite Duras, *Emily L.*

"Lesbian" and "Woman" interest me most when "Feminism" occupies the site of the conjunction, the colon as copula that seeks to balance the terms, to strike relationships between them which do not necessarily exist. I always write about the lesbian : woman as though she were a feminist, as if she (all three of us) occupied the same body. This improper speaking disturbs me as a way of defining the "lesbian" (body), as flesh or word. I suspect that impropriety marks every instance of speaking or writing about the lesbian, just as it does *the* body, *the* woman. In regard to this problematic of sexual identity and definition, Stephen Heath observes:

22

We exist as individuals in relation to and in the relations of language, the systems of meaning and representation in which, precisely, we find ourselves—try to imagine the question of who you are and any answer outside of language, outside of those systems. Sexual relations are relations through language, not to a given other sex; the body is not a direct immediacy, it is tressed, marked out, intrinsically involved with meanings. Of course, we can shake our heads, appeal to the fact that *we know* the direct experience of the body, two bodies in love, making love. Yet "direct experience," "the body" and so on are themselves specific constructions, specific notions; the appeal to which is never natural but always part of a particular system. (154)

What does this mean when applied to my lover's body? That I will never have "it," never write "it," approximating my lover's beauty only imperfectly in letters. But one thing I know: *we are dangerous*. Imperfections in the letter demand caution. The slip and slide of the signifying chain requires the lover's vigilance just as compellingly as her mouth and hands attend to her beloved when she makes love to her.

Letters are ill-suited to the body, to the "natural." As the Biographer in *Orlando* explains, taking the teenage writer's text as a subject:

He [Orlando] was describing, as all young poets are for ever describing, nature, and in order to match the shade of green precisely he looked (and here he showed more audacity than most) at the thing itself, which happened to be a laurel bush growing beneath the window. After that, of course, he could write no more. Green in nature is one thing, green in literature another. Nature and letters seem to have a natural antipathy; bring them together and they tear each other to pieces. (17)

In the postmodern, anti-romantic frame, the "liter-al" and the "letter-al" (differ(e/a)nce) are at war with one another. The belief in language's capacity to stand in for its subject, or to render the object a subject, is shattered but not forgotten; the operation of "meaning" is what is.

With respect to knowing and speaking the body, Rodolphe
Gasché comments, "Of the body—the body proper—we can
speak only improperly. So it will not only be necessary to talk
about it in metaphors, but also to develop the discourse of the
body, by a process of substitution, as a chain of figures amongst
others. Wishing to speak *of* the body, we can therefore only
speak of quite other things, to the point where we might ask
ourselves if the body does not consist precisely in those other
things, in that grouping of initially heterogeneous elements. In
which case the body would be dependent on a certain confusion,
because it is always more or less than a body properly speaking"
(3). There is no properly spoken body, no body properly speaking, it being always "more" or "less." We speak it improperly as
an always imperfect translation, a bad match of flesh and word,
but also as a violation of the law, its spirit if not its letter, identity
and language.

The body is a "sum(mary)" of the words accumulated to articulate it, more or less; Gasché continues, "the sum of the body
is the result of a selection, of an elimination (subtraction) of
many things. The only things selected to go into the sum(ma)
are of the sort that can be summarised in one's own sum"
(11). But according to some (sum), this body is never a sum,
never whole, always a hole; or, any/every textual body is an
imperfect body. In this sense, the lesbian (like the feminist,
the woman, and the text) has an improper body that fails
according to language's phallic measure. By all rights (writes),
man's textual, that is, his "liter-al" body is similarly deficient
or inadequate, but the (w)hole of woman's body is doubly
marked.[1]

"Difference"/"Differance"—e/a—what's the differ(e/a)nce? A
letter here, a letter there. When a woman chooses not to measure up, she can be a lesbian, and sometimes a feminist (if she
thinks of it in particular socio-cultural terms). She posts a letter,
"L," to those who care to read it. Every lesbian : woman might
be one.

Dear L—

Although these words appear and will reappear, remember that they were written in your name, just as Virginia and Vita wrote to one another.

Dear V—

Do you believe that desire is more interesting than consummation? And so we must become experts of deferral. Deferral—was it you or I who determined that?

V.

An agony inhabits deferred desire, the pain and excitement of letters writing tracks never finished word upon word: Can there be a meaning without consummation? But what ambiguity is there in the way my tongue traces ever so slowly gently the tip just meeting the surface of you fold by fold around whorl to whorl I follow the subtle turns of your ear wanting to take it all in at once seeking the dark of your certain desiring places enigmas just at the point where inner and outer meet, writing my way down your body letter after letter one formless ecstatic sound following another toward places we have not met before, that I only imagine we will discover, there first and there again. We wait always for the next time which will be the first time. Still, because not still at all, I know you understand just how these words feel on/in your body.

Love,
L

How to know you is the mystery I engage as your lover. It is installed at the heart of the lover's task, never finished, compelling vision and voice, moving tongue and hands.

"But could I ever know her?"—Virginia on Vita

Virginia Woolf's *Orlando: A Biography* (1928) has been called "the longest and most charming love letter in literature" (Nicolson 202). I like that. The lesbian love letter is a genre that I am inventing as I write.[2] Woolf dedicates her book "To V. Sackville-West." Her "dedication" to Vita precedes the text, an exergue, a going forth that suggests something before the letter of the text, that presents itself as an answer to Vita's letters, especially *Seducers in Ecuador* (1924), a study in the curiosity of vision, love letters, property and tradition, dedicated to Virginia four years earlier. It is another letter in the series of letters that constitutes their relationship, their "*epistolarium* of love" (Leaska, *Letters of VS-W* 27).[3] Something re-presents itself in these exchanges, where Michael Leaska's "virgin, shy, schoolgirlish" (really) Virginia so seductively engages Vita, "a grenadier, hard, handsome, manly" (Glendinning 128). An affection that the text as gift stands (in) for. Like true gifts, the text is something uncalled for, unexpected. A surprise of love. Love: a gift of what one does not have. (Vita to Virginia: "I wish, in a way, that we could put the clock back a year. I should like to startle you again —even though I didn't know then that you were startled" [*Letters* 151]. Or, as Virginia describes their sexual intimacy, "The night you were snared, that winter, at Long Barn [18 December 1925]" [*Letters* 301].) Through the agency of the letter, Virginia : Vita constitutes herself as subject, and startles her lover by desire's request that the lover make the asker a subject, not an object: "I try to invent you for myself, but find I really have only 2 twigs and 3 straws to do it with. I can get the sensation of seeing you—hair, lips, colour, height, even, now and then, the eyes and hands, but I find you going off, to walk in the garden, to play tennis, to dig, to sit smoking and talking, and then I can't invent a thing you say" (*Letters* 3:204–205). In other words, they take each other and themselves, through the lover/other, as subjects of desire, but also as objects, the beloved of the speaker/lover. As Brossard puts it, "a lesbian is . . . the centre of a captivating *image* which any woman can claim for herself" (*Aerial* 121). Through the letter, Woolf stakes out her claim.

Orlando begins with the qualified certainty of Orlando's sex as male: "He—for there could be no doubt of his sex, though the fashion of the time did something to disguise it—was in the act of slicing at the head of a Moor which swung from the rafters" (13). But "his" clothing poses an element of confusion, making it impossible to read sex "literally," as an indicator of sexual position. Woolf's narrator-Biographer, however, chooses to read from another position, the "unscientific" one of "riot and confusion of the passions and emotions" (16) where, for the speaker and the character, the sex and "nature" of others is not quite clear: "Ransack the language as he might, words failed him. . . . For in all she [Sasha, his beloved] said, however open she seemed and voluptuous, there was something hidden; in all she did, however daring, there was something concealed" (47). The implication of the concealed emerges as the shadowy other employed to produce the one.

In a sense, critical interest in androgyny in Woolf's work prepares us for and distracts us from (as it disguises) her lesbian interests—a diversionary tactic she deploys. Rachel Blau Du-Plessis describes Woolf's circumstances as follows: "Orlando is released into a space not only beyond narrative conventions but also beyond sexual norms. Lesbianism is the unspoken contraband desire that marriage liberates and that itself frees writing. The love of women appears with some circumspection, intermingled with the androgynous, ambisexual marriage and the doubled gender identities of Orlando" (63). Makiko Minow-Pinkney, Maria DiBattista and Francette Pacteau also shed light on the question. Minow-Pinkney regards the sex change in *Orlando* as a fantasy concerning "the transgression of boundaries as a play with the limit, as a play of difference" (122) enacting "alteration not resolution" or a Hegelian synthesis of the either/or to the static reification of "both" (131). Orlando swings from pole to pole "as if she belonged to neither [sex]; and indeed, for the time being she seemed to vacillate; she was man; she was woman; she knew the secrets, shared the weaknesses of each. It was a most bewildering and whirligig state of mind to be in" (158). The differences between the sexes elude specification in "pure" (as opposed to relational) terms, a phenomenon Woolf's text enacts as it moves through epochs and sexes: "It is a matter of where the dividing line is, and its location varies historically and socially. Any definition only has meaning in relation to a specific socio-historical context, since there is no innate bond between signifier and signified" (130). As such, then, the transgressions androgyny enacts, Minow-Pinkney maintains, "can only be presented in metonymical displacements, a sliding of one form into another" (131). These slips and slides, the hide-and-seek of how sexual identity can be represented, remain in motion, but the slide of "one form into another" depends upon preexisting types.

DiBattista views androgyny similarly, as "a double triumph. It overwhelms those stubborn, basically artificial divisions between men and women and thus discovers the basis of a legitimate social order governed by the law of equal association. And it also liberates the mind of women from the most enduring form of cultural and biological tyranny—the tyranny of sex!" (19). Androgyny is a way out of the either/or trap through the substitution of a both/and relationship. Arguing along similar lines, DuPlessis sees the "Orlando figure" as "both A and not-A, a logical contradiction, but a narratable prototype of constant heterogeneity" (*Writing* 63). According to DiBattista, the ruse of the "objective biographer" permits Woolf to "hide . . . the radical subjectivity and indeterminism that invariably attends the treatment of sex in social and political life and in fiction itself. Sex is not a fact, but a space in the psychic life, a hole or lapsus in identity onto which are projected the imagoes, archetypes, or stereotypes comprehended in terms male and female" (118). Pacteau presents a more complex, labile view of androgyny. It is and is not, because it vexes representation: "Androgyny can be said to belong to the domain of the imaginary, where desire is unobstructed; gender identity to that of the symbolic, the Law" (63). In other words, she calls the "some thing" that exceeds the law "androgyny."

Probably there are some limits and circumstances that desire does not know or recognize. It eludes apprehension, only finding itself, and that, sometimes obscurely, in the lover. How, then, can I know her, or even recognize who she is in me?

Dear L,

I have many pictures of you in various poses and moods, some when you don't know I am watching. I like those best, except when you are here and really looking at me instead of the lens. Now I look at pictures.

I have been waiting for your call, a reward for waiting. Just a sound is worth my attention. Such a small thing. But then we both know how it makes all the difference, begins to spin out the matrix of difference and meaning we live in. I am always so intent on hearing your voice, more lovely than Satie, etching tracks on the surface of memory like the tips of my fingers trying to memorize the smooth skin on your hand, your arms and back, to remember precisely the viscosity of fluid you when we make love. Fine calibrations of measure and degree, surface and interior distance. Ways of trying to know you/me/what it is we see in one another.

Love,
L

Starting again. The lesbian question is this: when Virginia looks at Vita, what does she see? What happens when a woman thinks of woman "in what is called 'that way' " (Vita, in Nicolson 29)? It is the question Rachel Bowlby as a feminist reader of Woolf fails to ask. Or that Michael Leaska answers in too literal and limited a way: "In the early months Virginia saw Vita as supple, savage, and patrician. To Vita, Virginia was the 'gentle genius'—lovely, idolized, and remote" (Leaska, *Letters* 11). This answer begs the question, saying nothing about attraction and affection between women, about lesbian relationship. Is the question—what does one "see" in the other—too personal, too speculative (from the Latin *specere*, to look at)? Another improper embodiment for the serious critical inquirer who would prefer not to look?

This is the difference between Bowlby, the feminist critic, who can write a chapter about *Orlando* without mentioning the word *lesbian*, and me. Or Nigel Nicolson who avoids the word in his affectionate "liberal"-minded description of *Orlando:* "The effect of Vita on Virginia is all contained in *Orlando*, the longest and most charming love letter in literature, in which she explores Vita, weaves her in and out of the centuries, tosses her from one sex to the other, plays with her, dresses her in furs, lace and emeralds, teases her, flirts with her, drops a veil of mist around her, and ends by photographing her in the mud at Long Barn, with dogs, awaiting Virginia's arrival next day" (218). I say it matters when a critic avoids (a form of suppression) the word lesbian; as long as the word matters, makes a social, political or artistic difference, it matters when *lesbian* is not spoken.

These critics also differ substantially from the more probing and explicit treatment of lesbianism Sherron Knopp offers in her essay, " 'If I Saw You Would You Kiss Me?': Sapphism and the Subversiveness of Virginia Woolf's *Orlando*"—an exploration in which Knopp, while refusing, unlike Blanche Wiesen Cook, to specify her relationship to their relationship, installs the lesbian subject at the center of her argument, as she claims, "Yet the extent to which Vita and Virginia did love each other— profoundly and, in every sense of the words, erotically and sexually (the frequency or infrequency with which they went to bed is irrelevant)—is something that continues to be resisted, denied, ignored, qualified out of significance, or simply unrecognized, even by the feminist revolution that enshrined Virginia as its saint" (24). The lesbian critic, "reading as a lesbian critic," reading "in *that* way," searches for something else and finds it, there in the sometimes silent language of the look between those two women, the space between words, the awesome passion of their engagement, even when they are (only) writing. Asking this improper question marks the lesbian scene or angle of vision, brings it into being. Virginia chooses to look, and sees. (Virginia to Vita: "and Vita is a dear old rough coated sheep dog: or alternatively, hung with grapes, pink with pearls, lustrous, candle lit"; *Letters* 79). This lesbian gaze is incompatible with Trautmann's de-sexualizing view of Virginia and Vita as cloistered nuns, a figure that is meant (before such explosive works as *The Three Marias* and *Lesbian Nuns: Breaking Silence*) to undercut the sensuality and eroticism of their lives and texts: "Part of both women's solitude, as discussed before, was an almost fierce sexlessness, or more accurately, a narcissistic sexuality, a state for contemplating themselves and their own feminine sensibilities, which at these times substituted in intensity for the erotic. In this solitude no man could get at them for a while. Both Vita and Virginia had this and other qualities of the cloistered nun" (32). The critical assortment of faulty or incomplete deductions and simple analogies produces the barren, imprisoned reading its figures lead us to make, as it runs counter to the playful eroticism in the desiring regard of one woman for another that marks these modern love letters as lesbian.

When Virginia looked at Vita, did she see Orlando/*Orlando?* What did she want? In 1928 she wrote to Vita, demanding her love through the imperative "first" choice:

> Love Virginia (imperative)
> Love Virginia (absolute)
> Love? Virginia? (interrogative)
> Mine was the 1st.
>   (*Letters* 3:446)

Did she discover, in this looking, a projection of indirection and inflection, a going and a return, or, in other words (her—Virginia's/Vita's?), "style"? In the process of writing *Orlando*, Virginia writes to Vita: "Shall I come Saturday for the night?—

seems the only chance. Let me know. . . . Should you say, if I rang you up to ask, that you were fond of me? If I saw you would you kiss me? If I were in bed would you—I'm rather excited about Orlando tonight: have been lying by the fire and making up the last chapter" (*Letters* 246). Orlando/Vita (who signs her name so, and to whom Virginia addresses other "love" letters), and *Orlando*, that novel inventing and commemorating Vita, excite Virginia. Are they separable? What's the differ(e/a)nce: Vita and Orlando, "Orlando" and Orlando or *Orlando*? As she completes her novel, Virginia is not certain: "The question now is, will my feelings for you be changed? I've lived in you all these months—coming out, what are you really like? Do you exist? Have I made you up?" (*Letters* 264).

Orlando/*Orlando* performs a trajectory of desire as it constructs and propels itself toward its desiderata, or as DeSalvo puts it, *Orlando* is "a book in which [Virginia] would possess Vita utterly" (204). But as Orlando's biographer notes, the meditation on love, that "first question," yields an unending metaphorics rather than the certainty of conclusion: "And as the first question had not been settled—What is love?—back it would come at the least provocation or none, and hustle Books or Metaphors or What one lives for into the margins, there to wait till they saw their chance to rush into the field again" (100). Line by line, desire marks out a future, or as the Biographer tells us three times on a page, "Life and a lover" (185). Concerning this mysterious trajectory, Lacan writes, "What counts is not that the other sees where I am, but that [s]he sees where I am going, that is to say, quite precisely, that [s]he sees where I am not. In every analysis of the intersubjective relation, what is essential is not what is there, what is seen. What structures it is what is not there" (*Seminar I* 224). This is true and not true, isn't it? Perhaps true only to the extent that we *are* interested in the "intersubjective relation" as Virginia pursues the volcanic Vesuvius, Vita (Glendinning 124). We want to see what she sees, to know how she wants to be seen. We also want to see what she cannot see, the "what is not there" of desire as she writes it.

Dear "Orlando"—

I reread all your letters today for signs of how, then, you knew that I would later stand in front of you showing my passion, that I will later still, though you already know it and knew it then, make love to you in words and ways you will forget only with great difficulty and after a long time. What wisdom is it that lets you write a future for me—seeing me where I was not yet, as I look at you now—that even I had not read for me and was powerless to invent. This must be the way that desire through its persistent longing makes what we will become for one another, as in the deferred space of love, a future consummation first imagines and then writes itself as it waits for us to take ourselves down full length, length to length, our bodies finally side by side one on the other and again, searching for the points, compelling the intersection where two no longer feel like two, subject and object indistinct, as with my eyes closed I cannot tell my pleasure from yours, and begin to feel that certain ecstasy we are learning to become in one another.

Love,
V.

Pacteau argues that "Fantasy, rooted in the absence of an object, is contingent upon a distance; that between viewer and viewed, where the unconscious comes to rest, along which look and psyche travel" (77–78). The complex intersection of observer and observed—in an intricate fabric of desire, in an erotics of en-gaze-ment—recalls Barthes's exploration of the ecstasy of the gaze, as the object pierces the subject in an ecstatic confusion of activity and passivity. Jane Gallop explains, "Ecstasy etymologically derives from the Greek *ekstasis*, from *ex-*, 'out,' plus *histanai*, 'to place.' Thus, it means something like 'placed out.' Ecstasy is when you are no longer within your own frame: some sort of going outside takes place" (15). Barthes calls this excessive ecstatic pleasure *jouissance;* Orlando/ the Biographer/ Virginia sums it up in "Ecstasy! . . . Ecstasy!" (287); "Laughter, Laughter!" (271); "Life, Life, Life!" (270)—the Latin translation of which, Leaska points out, becomes "Vita, Vita, Vita!" (46), the lover's signature.

"I try to invent you for myself."—Virginia on Vita

"For myself." "You" for "me." That there is an "I" and a "you," has great import. As Peggy Kamuf explains, "If there is to be a coming together in a convention of meaning, 'I' and 'you' cannot be subsumed into only an 'I.' By itself, in other words, 'I' makes no sense. There is no meaning, no contract without the more-than-one of an 'I/you' articulated by their difference" (53). Vita writes from Teheran that she wants a picture of Virginia and asks if her own has turned up: "It is a torment not being able to visualize when one wants to. I can visualize you as a matter of fact surprisingly well,—but always as you stood on your doorstep that last evening, when the lamps were lit and the trees misty, and I drove away" (*Letters* 112). Virginia saw in Vita the spec(tac)ular image of herself, of Virginia the lesbian lover. She invents the lesbian woman who loves women, who might love her, whom she might love. Through speculation, surmise and even imagination, Woolf, like Orlando's biographer, attempts "to elucidate a secret that has puzzled historians for a hundred years": to fill in the "hole in the manuscript [record of Orlando's life] big enough to put your finger through" (119). She invents herself as she writes the other, or as Linda Kauffman puts it in her probing work on epistolarity and desire, "Since every letter to the beloved is also a self-address, . . . the heroine's project—aided by her reading and her writing—also involves self-creation, self-invention" (25). Through the Biographer and Vita, Woolf constructs herself as a lesbian of letters at the same time that she gives us the lesbian in letters. But who *is* "she"?

Dear V—
    You invite perceptual study:

Parallax, n. [Gr. *parallaxis*, from *parallas sein*, to vary, to decline or wander; *para*, beyond, and *allassein*, to change.]

PARALLAX

P, star; R, point on earth's surface; A,
center of the earth; angle RPA, parallax

1. the apparent change in the position of an object resulting
   from the change in the direction or position from which it is
   viewed.
2. the amount or angular degree of such change; specifically, in
   astronomy, the apparent difference in the position of a heav-
   enly body with reference to some point on the surface of the
   earth and some other point, as the center of the earth (*diurnal*, of *geocentric, parallax*) or a point on the sun (*annual*, or
   heliocentric, parallax): the parallax of an object may be used
   in determining its distance from the observer.

—Webster's New World Dictionary

What is the parallax of you, the graceful angle we compose of
you me surface and center, seen in this way, a bright star that
suddenly changes direction in the night sky, a new sun I gradu-
ally alter myself to see. Was it you who moved or I, standing
now in a shy ecstasy (mine and yours) at the door as you come
up the walk, your head turned eyes slightly angled toward me
waiting through the distance between years the night the morning hours slowly assembling themselves with diurnal regularity
toward such an orderly vision, like the way my words ultimately
compose themselves on the page, toward the feel of you.

Love,
L

The parallax distance is a function of the view, the coursing of desire, the elaboration of fantasy. Pacteau explains the figure of the androgyne in similar terms: "The androgyne dwells in a distance. The androgynous figure has to do with *seduction*, that which comes before undressing, seeing, touching. It can only exist in the shadow area of an image; once unveiled, once we throw a light on it, it becomes a woman or man, and I (myself) resume my position on the side of the female. The perfect symmetry of the figure of the androgyne positions the viewer at the convergence of the feminine and the masculine where 's/he' oscillates. The androgyne is excessive in its transgression of the boundaries of gender identity; however, this threat of super-abundance, of overflowing, is safely contained within the frame of the feminine and the masculine" (78–79). The androgyne, as a gap, an excess, resembles the lesbian, but without community, without the socio-politics of identity and the history of move-ment and struggle, and is still caught within the oppositional categories of gender. The androgyne, as such, then, is the "first figure," but s/he is a figure in motion, the "origin" that never was, a potential only to be re-figured or given over to the either/ or. The androgyne, as/when represented, according to Pacteau, shows (up) "as an attempt to objectify desire, to reduce into one *still* image a process, is in itself contrary to the dynamics of the fantasy that produces it. . . . Representation of the androgynous 'in between' is an impossibility. Perhaps it is because of the image's overwhelming concern with the 'body' as the site of all truth. The 'body' as an entity, as an end in itself, cannot contain the excess of the androgynous fantasy" (81).

Letters, like all texts, but love letters in particular as a signed pledge from me to you, leave "the door open for all sorts of improprieties and expropriations" (Kamuf 25); as Kamuf ex-plains, there "is no guarantee that [s/]he [the signer] feels what [s/]he expresses or expresses what [s/]he feels" (25). (Vita to Virginia: "Do you ever mean what you say, or say what you mean? or do you just enjoy baffling the people who try to creep a little nearer?" *Letters* 52) What ever does the letter—L, for example—mean?

In/through Orlando/*Orlando*, Virginia becomes (most like) Vita; she imagines her (as) lover, her love affair. When she began the book, she wrote to Vita, "Yesterday morning I was in despair. . . . I couldn't screw a word from me; and at last dropped my head in my hands: dipped my pen in the ink, and wrote these words, as if automatically, on a clean sheet: Orlando: A Biography. No sooner had I done this than my body was flooded with rapture and my brain with ideas. I wrote rapidly till 12. . . . But listen; suppose Orlando turns out to be Vita; and its *[sic]* all about you and the lusts of your flesh and the lure of your mind (heart you have none, who go gallivanting down the lanes with [Mary] Campbell) . . . Shall you mind? Say yes, or No: . . ." (*Letters* 237). On these grounds, Françoise Defromont argues that *Orlando* is a public exposé of Vita's affections and infidelities, and Virginia's jealousy, which she displaces in/through writing (185). Similarly, Knopp describes the novel as both "public proclamation" and private exploration: "Far from being a way to create distance in the relationship, *Orlando* was a way to heighten intimacy—not a substitute for physical lovemaking but an extension of it" (27). A love affair of the letter (when I inscribe the words on the paper, I get excited).

We could say that Virginia saw herself and not herself, herself as she wished to be-come (that is, a woman like the Vita she saw), herself as she wished Vita to see her (a woman Vita could love), and Vita as Virginia wished her to be, the one who puts Virginia on the "first rung of her ladder." Virignia sees, first and foremost, a lesbian, and invests in Vita, through the character of Orlando, the history of women "like" her—500 years of lesbianism, or 400 years of English tradition—one of Woolf's most striking realizations, and the very awareness that produces (itself) in the curious construction of Orlando, larger than life, longer than life, all of life.

Vita responds to the experience of *Orlando* by remarking that it gives a new meaning to narcissism: "you have invented a new form of Narcissism,—I confess,—I am in love with Orlando—this is a complication I had not foreseen" (*Letters* 289). Virginia/ Orlando/ Vita. Desire, according to Lacan, is always triangulated, but I see Virginia/Vita–Orlando/Virginia/Vita–Virginia/ Leonard; Vita–Virginia/Violet/Rosamund–Harold. Father : mother/ lover/ daughter.

Vita's image returns (her) to herself. But it is Virginia's narcissism as well—an auto-erotic gesture (loving one's self enough to create a lover), a self-engendering move (becoming lesbian, beloved and beloved), a creation of one's (and one's self as) lover and love object,[4] a brilliant circuitry. A "writer's holiday," "an escapade" (*WD* 117–18, 124), Orlando/*Orlando* is a love affair.

Dear V—

My lover is a writer. She makes secret turns of phrase and tongue as she inscribes me, (re)writing my love for her. How her text makes me trace my passion on her body, how she (trans)forms me into her perfect lover she will not explain. Is it the writer who (be)comes the lover, or the other way around? I cannot say. She will not tell me. Sometimes she says that I am the one making (up) this intimate story, the title of which is "L," the subtitle and author for the moment unknown—*inconnu*, secret, clandestine, but very very beautiful.

Love,

L

"intimate letters"—Virginia to Vita (*Letters* 3:117)

In writing *Orlando*, Virginia Woolf set out to make an intimate story very public, or perhaps it was to make a public story very intimately her own. She wrote in her diary on October 22, 1927: "I am writing *Orlando* half in a mock style very clear and plain, so that people will understand every word. But the balance between truth & fantasy must be careful" (*Diary* 3:162). As Defromont contends in *Virginia Woolf, Vers la maison de lu-*

mière, Woolf's texts explore the relation between life, writing and libidinal energy, "between talent and femininity, emotion and art" (171). *Flush*, the biography of Elizabeth Barrett Browning's spaniel, most pointedly displays this investigation (61–62). Woolf struggles between the poles of intellect and instinct, the differ(e/a)nce constitutive of *jouissance* in both instances (137).

In *Signature Pieces*, Kamuf suggests a way of describing the relationship between Virginia and her lover Vita and the text or letter/character of Orlando, or *Orlando*. Kamuf writes provocatively that the signature is "an always divisible limit within the difference between writer and work, 'life' and 'letters.' Signature articulates the one with the other, the one *in* the other: it both divides and joins. It is this double-jointedness of signatures that will be lost to any discourse that continues to posit an essential exteriority of subjects to the texts they sign" (viii). Thus the problematic of lesbian : writing is inscribed in what Defromont describes as the "or/and, *Or/l/and/*o)" (209), the passage from one sex to the other, one writing function to the next. *Orlando* is (a) play on words, on/in the letter. The signature "is the mark of an articulation at the border between life and letters, body and language. An articulation both joins and divides; it joins and divides identity with/from difference. A difference from itself, within itself, articulates the signature on the text it signs" (Kamuf 39–40). It joins and divides "the historically singular subject to which it refers (or seems to refer) and the formal generality of language" (Kamuf 41).

Desire writes the absence in/of its heart, a lack, as Lacan puts it, "beyond anything which can represent it. It is only ever represented as a reflection on a veil" (*Seminar II* 223), the shadowy hand on a fine sheet of paper or the faint tracks on the sheets after rising, inscribing the love letter. Will I be able to read it? The Biographer cautions us that "the most poetic is precisely that which cannot be written down. For which reasons we leave a great blank here, which must be taken to indicate that the space is filled to repletion" (253). How do I see what Viginia sees? How do I see her seeing Vita? In a sense, "the

Biographer" tells me how to imagine Virginia looking at Vita, a gap and an overflow. And my lover and I (re)enact the scene/ seen.

Dear L—

It is you startled I see in the near distance eyes opened and my fluid love for you begins to move, the shudders of desire rush over me, lap on lap. Orlando sees the woman s/he loves and thinks of names—melon, pineapple, olive tree, emerald, the clear-eyed fox startled as it crosses the snow (37). These names the senses supply to construct their desire in the lover, to approximate "the green flame [that] seems hidden in the emerald, or the sun prisoned in a hill" (47).

What names do I have for that desiring lover whose dark eyes are haunted with me, who is startled by the love we make together, whose surprise takes me by surprise, leads me to invent something more. Leads me to recall that other time at Long Barn where one woman startled another in love, and then to plot a narrative in which we all invent our parts. Invention— the events, the feelings, the names for the words that fail to speak what is hidden, concealed in the ways we move in one another, how much we want it in the space of deferral, whether we are together or apart.

This letter locates us side by side, puts us here in the same place, even though I know you are away, that I must wait for your return as I construct my desire in memory of your body. It must be the lover's work to write love letters, character after character, arranging the white spaces and the dark shapes, forms of silence and sound, presence and absence, hour after hour, with the same careful attention she pays to her lover's body, as she waits for her to come back so she can put this letter aside and lead her to the bedroom, take off her clothes, arrange her gently but ever so quickly on the bed and continue together with a violent tenderness to compose their love in gestures and sounds that have no easy names, shapes that come to us from a place beyond meaning, or memory.

Love,

L

Like Woolf, who first places Chloe and Olivia in the laboratory, and then sees their differences (from one another, two women who are not waiting for men but for each other, an economy of difference not lack, not sameness; and their sufficiency, not waiting for a man to fulfill them, to fill them up, to plug up the w/hole so the body can be summed up).[5] She sees their secret, hers and mine, or at least the possibility of a future for them. In Vita, she sees herself loving Vita (her); she sees lesbian : woman. Her lesbian feminist readers see it too, and some feminist readers can learn to recognize the figure as well. Virginia writes to Vita about a woman who sent her a letter: "A woman writes that she has to stop and kiss the page when she reads O. —Your race I imagine. The percentage of Lesbians is rising in the States, all because of you" (*Letters* 318). More writing : more lesbians.

Dear Vita and Virginia,

How can I read your letters without, above all, wanting to write? Years of correspondence, circulating affection and longing make me desire more letters. I don't want them to end or to stop, so I continue (y)our correspondence.

Dear V, Your sheepdog puts her muzzle on her paws and waits at the door. Will you pet her when you arrive? Will you remember the feel of her fur and discover new ways to startle her? Love, V.

Dear V and V, I feel empty when I write one without the other. Even the letter V—one side an obverse mirroring of the other, only connected at that precise swelling point. There must be a name for this effect—V. In any case, it reads like a lesbian effect; a lesbian can claim it as her own. (Y)ours is, after all, "a captivating image."

V V V V V V V V V V V V V V V V V V V V

Taking flight,
Love,
L

THREE

A Crisis of Style—Re:Finding
Djuna Barnes's Nightwood

So far, when I have been mentioned, it has always been unfortunate and without exactitude.

—Djuna Barnes to Virginia Spencer Carr

A successful work . . . is not one which resolves objective contradictions in a spurious harmony, but one which expresses the idea of harmony negatively, by embodying the contradictions, pure and uncompromised, in its innermost structures.

—Theodor Adorno, *Prisms*

And when you see a woman who's broken
  Put her all into your arms
Cause we don't know where we come from
  We don't know what we are.

—Laurie Anderson, "Ramon," *Strange Angels*

In a collection called *Mon héroine* Nicole Brossard, the Quebec lesbian writer, selected Djuna Barnes, best known for the novel *Nightwood,* as her heroine-subject. Brossard notes some connections between them: in 1923 Barnes published a work called *A Book,* and in 1970, forty-seven years later, Brossard published her own work called *Un livre,* or *A Book.* We can take such a remarkable iterability as the sign of a lesbian : writing tradition. There are other signs. Michèle Causse, a French lesbian writer and friend of Brossard's, translated Barnes's *Ladies Almanack* into French, and Monique Wittig translated *Spillway,* a collection of Barnes's stories. Like Brossard, Causse and Wittig have also written on Barnes. How and by whom Barnes is both remembered and forgotten has interested me for a long time, since my first publication—another sign of lesbian relations.

The elusive Barnes is difficult to pin down, and efforts to do so seem con/founded. A significant difference exists between the awe and respect accorded her by these French and *quebecoise* writers and some notable critics of lesbian writing in the United States. In *Surpassing the Love of Men*, Lillian Faderman, for example, locates Barnes in relation to writers in the French tradition such as Renée Vivien who, she claims, internalized the images of lesbians served up in French "aesthete-decadent literature" (362–63). Faderman says of *Nightwood*, "The nineteenth-century views of lesbian narcissism and frustration are delivered up whole here" (364). Faderman blames Proust for these images, as well as Barnes, except in the *Ladies Almanack*, for not differentiating between the literary (predominantly male) view of lesbians and the lives of "real" lesbians she knew in the Barney circle: "Insane passion and degradation and doll games and roles had nothing to do with those women's conceptions of lesbianism" (364–65).[1] In her brief history of the background of contemporary lesbian culture and literature, Bonnie Zimmerman is equally dismissive of Barnes, also linking her to Vivien: "But Renée Vivien (like Djuna Barnes, author of the modernist classic *Nightwood* [1936]), borrowed her image of Sappho and lesbians from the exotic 'femme damnée,' intoxicated with death and lust" (6). Zimmerman accords Natalie Clifford Barney and Radclyffe Hall the more privileged positions in the narrative of lesbian literary tradition that is to follow: "Natalie Barney, virtually unique in her era, declined both the damnation of Renée Vivien [who, remember, is coupled with Barnes] and the codes of Gertrude Stein" (7). Hall, who gives us Barney's story in *The Well of Loneliness*, is, Zimmerman acknowledges, a much less accomplished writer than many others—Woolf, Stein, and Barnes among them. How could a tradition—or what kind of a tradition could—derive from Hall as "the most profound and lasting influence on modern-day notions of lesbians"? One that conforms to the far from antithetical romantic and social realist needs of a community: "for all its old-fashioned rhetoric about 'inversion' and its stylistic infelicities," Zimmerman claims, *The Well of Loneliness* never obscures its central premise that homosexuals deserve a place within nature and society" (7). The novel is a tear-jerker with a strong plot, a heroic protagonist—"an old-fashioned, readable novel" (7).

Another curious complication emerges from Zimmerman's analysis of the bleak time between 1928 when *The Well* was published and 1969, the year marking the consolidation of gay liberation. Despite the repressive social forces at work during that interim period, Zimmerman observes that "hidden, underground gay communities survived in large urban centers. Centered around bars and private friendship networks, they formed a substitute that, as the language of the time reminds us, existed 'in the shadows' or 'in the twilight world,' but not in the bright, open light of day" (8–9). The underground, the worlds of night and marginality, shadows and liminality—that's Barnes territory. The lesbians depicted in the many works of the '50s and '60s were viewed "as tragic, maimed creatures trapped in a world of alcohol, violence, and meaningless sex. The plots either doomed them to a cycle of unhappy love affairs or redeemed them through heterosexual marriage" (9), characteristics recalling the charges against Barnes. The few "best of these stories portrayed lesbians as strong and independent women, and thus indicated the feminist direction that lesbian politics and literature were to take" (Zimmerman 8). I wonder if the "*best* stories" are the "best *stories*," if a story has to offer a strong, independent lesbian in order to be good. If the ideological prerequisite serves as an aesthetic criterion (a kind of prescription for "good" lesbian : writing), then there probably is little room for Barnes, and maybe even Woolf and Stein, in charting our lesbian-feminist cultural heritage in the United States.

Also perplexing is the (dis)connection of Wittig and Barnes in the narratives of lesbian literary history. Zimmerman points to Wittig as one of the sources for the development of the political or theoretical position of lesbian feminism in the '70s and '80s, a position which "combined a commitment to female integrity, bonding, and sexual passion with an uncompromising rejection of male-centered ways of thinking and being. In place of these old ways, lesbian feminism presented a perspective from the margins of patriarchal society, a point of view rooted in women's forbidden love and desire for one another. Lesbian feminists proposed, therefore, that the word 'lesbian' *stood for* a specific relationship to the dominant society rather than simply being a name for women who 'happen' to make love to other women" (11). What is it, then, that some of the most radical lesbian feminist writers—Bertha Harris, for example—see in Djuna Barnes? How could Wittig and Brossard admire such a throw-back to masculinist, repressive, negative images of lesbians when neither of them produce such images themselves? And why haven't we asked this question before?

Dear L,

My heroine(s). It's hard for me to think this way, but you can surely be one. I need a long catalogue of women's names, like Wittig's in *Les Guérillères*. My history, finally invented. A lesbian genealogy: Woolf, Barnes, Stein, Wittig, Lorde, Causse, Brossard, Anzaldua, Nestle. Especially the last six—those who never deny the word, even as they struggle with its definitions.

I need to write Nicole about her heroine Djuna Barnes. She first read *Nightwood* in 1979, but I wonder if, when she wrote *Un livre,* she already knew of Barnes's pre-text, *A Book.* I think that then, in 1970, Nicole already "knew" her without knowing her. Did she call herself a lesbian then? When I first read *Nightwood,* I was a lesbian without knowing it. But I recognized a world in it—a scene over the edge, the night world of the different, my world. I wonder if a lesbian exists who didn't, at one time or another, begin here. An obscurity, exciting and terrifying.

Waiting to hear from you, love,

L

Another turn in the narratives of lesbian criticism further complicates the assessment of Barnes's influence. In "Zero Degree Deviancy: The Lesbian Novel in English," Catharine R. Stimpson mentions Barnes twice—early in the essay, comparing *The Well* to *Nightwood,* a better written "parable of damnation" (101), and at the end, citing Bertha Harris's devotion to Barnes. Stimpson's treatment of Hall, however, sheds light on the politics of a lesbian literary tradition. Hall, she reminds us, did not depict her personal pleasure either when she constructed Stephen Gordon, the tragic invert of *The Well:* "In brief, *The Well of Loneliness* tends to ignore the more benign possibilities of lesbianism. Hall projects homosexuality as a sickness. To deepen the horror, the abnormal illness is inescapable, preordained; an ascribed, not an achieved status" (101). While acceptance might be sought in heaven since the lesbian, in this reading, is justified or rationalized as a divine creation, it is rarely to be found on earth; such, in any case, Hall claims in *The Well.*

What plays itself out in recent lesbian literary histories is the politics of modern aesthetic judgment. Surely it is no accident that some of the most difficult (not "readable"?) of our contemporary writers admire the experimental writers who came before them. Zimmerman, in an interesting discussion of lesbian writing of the last two decades, notes that, as a result of an internalized censor, "much lesbian fiction exhibits a subtle or not-so-subtle party line, avoids satire and irony, and is ambivalent about the imagination and experimentation. . . . Writers today write for a community that wants its fiction accessible, entertaining, and just 'correct' enough to be a bit bland" (19). Satire, irony, imagination and experimentation—the writer's stock and trade.

"*Satire*—A literary manner that blends a critical attitude with HUMOR and WIT for the purpose of improving human institutions or humanity. True satirists are conscious of the frailty of institutions and attempt through laughter not so much to tear them down as to inspire a remodeling" (Holman and Harmon 447).

"*Irony*—[A] figure of speech in which the actual intent is expressed in words that carry the opposite meaning. . . . Its presence is marked by a sort of grim HUMOR and 'unemotional detachment' on the part of the writer, a coolness in expression at a time when the writer's emotions appear to be really heated" (Holman and Harmon 264).

"*Imagination*—While *imagination* is usually viewed as a 'shaping' and ordering power, the function of which is to give art its special authority, the assumption is almost always present that the 'new' creation shaped by the *imagination* is a new form of reality, not a FANTASY or a fanciful project" (Holman and Harmon 250–51).

Experimentation—XX % XX @@@ XX OoO **** OoO XXX (How to say *I love you/I miss you*.)

Lesbian readers, in other words, want their literature "straight"—tested and true, signifier and signified tightly stitched, direct and to the point. Surely otherwise the social criticism of satire, the passion underwriting irony, and the (re)inventive impulses fueling imagination and experimentation would be viewed as appropriate, even desirable, for a lesbian or a lesbian-feminist writing.

Despite Zimmerman's view of *The Well of Loneliness* as a landmark text for contemporary lesbian writers, Stimpson's argument that it is, like *Nightwood*, another lesbian damnation tale, compels us to look elsewhere (that is, beyond plot resolution and character type) to account for Barnes's relatively limited reception. It seems reasonable to suspect that she is neglected less for political than aesthetic reasons since her writing signals a departure from the romantic/naturalistic/realistic norms that dominate literature in the twentieth century. Cheryl Plumb's contention that Barnes chose to work more in the tradition of the French symbolists, and I would add, on through to the decadents, suggests one possible rationale. Certainly this heritage echoes in Zimmerman and Faderman's assessments, which we could extend to say that Barnes's writing more nearly resembles the tradition of Baudelaire than it does Zola, or as Marcus demonstrates, we could trace Barnes through Hugo to Rabelais ("Laughing" 225).

In critiquing bourgeois values, the French symbolists, of necessity, attacked the form of the novel as well. Their experimentalism was, Plumb explains, "designed to force a new kind of consciousness. Such an aesthetic demanded from the reader vigilance and reconstruction of meaning; the reader as collaborator" (16). Barnes could have made it easier for us, just as she might have had an easier relation to life as a source for imaginative material. She could have found in naturalism the determinism that produces the "invert" or the "deviant"; at issue, in other words, is a matter of design not talent. She could have given us an acceptable moral cloaked in a "readable" story (her success as a journalist underscores this possibility). Barnes's complexity, suggested by what is given and what is withheld, has long been recognized by some of her more attentive readers. Louis F. Kannenstine attributes the difficulty to three sources: "a poetic style . . . us[ing] image and symbol in a modern way, that is, by multiplication of connotations through contextual variation; an oblique approach to narrative which, distrusting linear progression of action and chronological character development, reveals the timeless undercurrent life of its characters; and a tendency . . . to imply rather than directly elaborate the themes" (xiv). More trouble. Multi-plication rather than simplification or direct correspondence between word and idea, variation, implication rather than direction: obliquity.

"*Obliquity*—1. the state or quality of being oblique; 2. an oblique statement, action, etc.; 3. a turning aside from moral conduct or sound thinking; 4. *Astron.* the orbit around the sun, approximately 23° 27' and

decreasing at the rate of o.47" a year; 5. *Math.* a) deviation of a line or plane from the perpendicular or parallel; b) the degree of this."
—*Webster's New World Dictionary*

Although lesbian readers call for lesbian writers to "tell it like it is" (Zimmerman 23–24), things are not always what they seem, nor do they always seem to be what they are. Obliquity. Parallax. Fluid you/me.

It shouldn't surprise us that readers of French, those familiar with the milieu within which Barnes wrote, were much more appreciative of her experimentalism even before the recent post-structuralist shift altered critical perspectives. But the question remains: what do these "other" lesbian readers find in Barnes's *Nightwood*—that crooked, obliquely leaning text, a deviation in the letter? In answer, we could begin by regarding *Nightwood* as an analog for the "lesbian" as read by "straight" readers (lesbian or not), that is, those who want to read books that "tell it like it is." The equation is simple: the "other" lesbian reader is to the "straight" lesbian reader as *Nightwood* is to the "tell it like it is" novel. In some quarters, it is an outcast, placed on the margins, so that its difference frees us from taking it into account as we attempt to plot a diverse lesbian literary heritage. The novel's treatment, in other words, resembles that of sadomasochism within feminism, an issue many lesbian writers feel is always best left for some other time, as the texts of Black, Native, Hispanic and Asian women were omitted earlier in feminist discussion of writing and tradition.[2]

I believe Brossard reads just such a marginalization in *Nightwood*, but she describes it differently, by saying that Barnes advances the problematics of women's ontological existence (*Héroine* 200). Registered in these terms, Brossard's admiration, like Barnes's text, goes unaccounted for. Perhaps more importantly for these lesbian writers, Barnes engages the most pressing subject of all—the lesbian imagination as it writes the convergence of the literary and the amatory projects (200, 203), the love quest for/in the letter. Brossard and Wittig find in Barnes the very point of the lesbian desire to see life as it is, which is the desire to see oneself there, to read, as one might read *Orlando,* a lesbian love letter. Thus, Wittig begins "The Point of View," by telling us that she has collected "reflections on writing and language . . . which are related to Djuna Barnes' work and to my own work" (63). Barnes's lesbian obliquity, her fracturing, "out-of-the-corner-of-the-eye perception" (65), stirs Wittig's imagination.

Barnes, Brossard, Wittig and I come together (you are invited too; it's not an exclusive company) through an interest in the relation of the (lesbian) letter to meaning. Writing a text with a homosexual theme involves "taking the risk that at every turn the formal element which is the theme will overdetermine the meaning, monopolize the whole meaning, against the intention of the author who wants above all to create a literary work" (65). The text tries to become a manifesto, "a committed text with a social theme," and it stops being art. Wittig explains, "When this happens to a text, it is diverted from its primary aim, which is to change the textual reality within which it is inscribed" ("Point" 65). She sees in this threat Barnes's dread of becoming a writer for lesbians (only).

Dear L,

Do you think a lesbian : writing by definition makes a difference in language? In my letters to you, do I reproduce the same old relation so that it almost doesn't matter that we are lesbians?

It doesn't seem possible to make (a) criticism that is about textual relations rather than "meaning." That's why this text remains erotic criticism (if either term works for you) rather than critical eroticism. The difference resides in the argument; otherwise, where would it be? Out the window, or maybe I can put it in the window, the place in my computer for consideration, revision, but not commitment. If I were to open several windows at once, I could materialize polysemy before your very eyes, shed some light on/in the subject.

> I love Djuna. . . .

> I don't want to live like Djuna. . . .

> I am frightened by Djuna. . . .

If we were to change our relationship, I would ask you to tell me here, in writing, what you really want to have happen between us. With a remarkable grace, I would say go, (because) I love you. Not out of some romantic magnanimity—the kind that comes from guilt or sacrifice, or even self-aggrandizement, but in the hope, of course, that you will choose me anyway, that I am what you want. In fact, us. But this isn't different, is it? Haven't we said these things before, and aren't we free to want this now?

I need to write something here, to make a letter, that I do not yet understand. Once I understand it, it seems, the textual relation will no longer be new. What is it that brings a letter to crisis, that exposes the terror? Therein lies the brilliance of Djuna Barnes. She writes what we had never known we felt before. She faces it down. And lives.

Love,

L

Barnes's *Nightwood* illustrates the prospects for lesbian writers who shift from naturalistic renderings of lesbianism, as in *The Well of Loneliness*, to begin to figure a new psychology of lesbian consciousness which displaces clinical categories of deviance. Building on Andrew Field's notion that Barnes's oeuvre reflects "deep auto-analysis" (98), we could say that she instructs us with the wisdom of the autodidact. Constructing herself (and/ as) her lesbian subject, she invents a grammar, syntax and lexicon of passion, grief and the painful limits of human understanding. O'Connor's comment to Frau Mann aptly serves as one of the novel's emblems: " 'I tell you, Madame, if one gave birth to a heart on a plate, it would say "Love" and twitch like the lopped leg of a frog' " (26–27). Thus, Kannenstine reminds us that "[i]t is the agony of the heart that remains when the mind comes up against mystery" (126)—so profoundly the case in *Nightwood*, and perhaps also paradigmatically the case of a lesbian writing that does not pretend to know.

Despite the disclaimers of James Scott and Barnes herself, *Nightwood* is a lesbian novel. While it may be other things as well, *Nightwood* places before the Hemingways of the world a life they would rather, like Jake Barnes in *The Sun Also Rises*, strike out at, deny or defame. Robin Vote, as the emerging lesbian subject, is composed with the care and regularity of syntactical arrangement, the lesbian body (di)splayed for our regard: "Her legs, in white flannel trousers, were spread as in a dance, the thick-lacquered pumps looking too lively for the arrested step. Her hands, long and beautiful, lay on either side of her face" (34). Barnes pushes the subject of the lesbian body back to mythic and physical emergence, the liminality of the border between being and not-being, "converging halves of a broken fate" (38) between the animal and the human, the lesbian and the heterosexual, the captivated and the lost: "The perfume that her body exhaled was of the quality of that earth-flesh fungi, which smells of captured dampness and yet is so dry, overcast with the odour of oil of amber, which is an inner malady of the sea, making her seem as if she had invaded a sleep incautious and entire. Her flesh was the texture of plant life, and beneath it one sensed a frame, broad, porous and sleep-worn, as if sleep were a decay fishing her beneath the visible surface" (34). *Nightwood*, in this sense, is a precursor of, a fore-play for Wittig's later works, the sensuality of *Les Guérillères* and the anatomical dissection of the lesbian subject in *The Lesbian Body*. In Robin Vote, the lesbian : reader meets herself, either coming or going.

The novel's title, Field reminds us (212), must have pleased Barnes when Eliot proposed it: NIGHTWOOD. The name reconstitutes the lover, textualizes her, installs her in the dark world of loss, longing and desire. THELMA WOOD. A cry in the night. Remember Barnes's claim: " 'I'm not a lesbian. I just loved Thelma' " (Broe, ed., *Silence and Power* 16). In *Nightwood*, the words operate like searchlights, although Joseph Frank claims that the chapters are "searchlights, probing the darkness" (31). In any case, a territory is surveyed. The text takes the shape of an underworld portrait gallery populated with subliminal versions of the selves we don't wish to recognize: the transvestite, the somnambule, the mother, the liar, the prognosticator, the wandering Jew. The prose arrests, glances over, and passes on again only to return, as Barnes illuminates her subject. The "anatomy of night," the book's initial subtitle, suggests the lesbian subject as an unwritten darkness, a silence cast in tableaux, just as we first meet Robin arrested in the dance of sleep, in the process of a move between "there" and "here," between the worlds of marriage and motherhood, and lesbian love and failed engagement. Nightwood. What is the night? The night world, night wood, bitter wood/world. "The night wood," according to Kannenstine, "is the medium for recurrence of all lost phenomena" (125). Robin, in *Nightwood*, recognizes an/ other contract.

Based on Thelma Wood, Robin is Barnes's loss, not just Nora's. Unlike Nora, who roams back streets and searches the dark corners of bars looking for Robin—"She sees her everywhere," O'Connor says (61), Barnes pursues "Robin," the absent lover, through the letter, through the pages of *Nightwood*. They do what any distraught lover does. But it is the reader that Barnes consigns to an endless search, seeking an explanation for loving and that slippage of the letter, losing, trying to come to terms with the terms of a new relationship to the letter. The eroticism of crisis, darkness, loss, longing and terror, under pressure of control, the structures of language and sense. While Robin's detachment infuriates us, Nora's unrelenting search embarrasses us. She is a literalist, a believer in "the word" (51). O'Connor observes that women like Nora scurry through the night in search of their lovers: "Like a thousand mice they go this way and that, now fast, now slow, some halting behind doors . . . all approaching or leaving their misplaced mouse-meat that lies in some cranny, on some couch, down on some floor, behind some cupboard; and all the windows, great and small, from which love and fear have peered, shining and in tears. Put those windows end to end and it would be a casement that would reach around the world; and put those thousand eyes into one eye and you would have the night combed with the great blind searchlight of the heart" (93). The dark erotics of the letter in *Nightwood* issues from the anfractuous, unrelenting quest for the love(r) not there, the non-rational passion on the brink of the just barely human. The lover's absence occasions the other's desire and propels her into the darkness, but there is a certain shame attached to the project: Robin, in her absence, "was an amputation that Nora could not renounce" (59). The reader, off on her own quest, participates in the erotic tension of the search, the wandering, the speculation, as she rides the sonorous vibrancy of the letter and pulsates with the electrical dynamism of the text's syntactical movement.

The novel presents a world in which people refuse identification and transference. They resist connection. Their passions are incommunicable, as O'Connor explains to Felix: "One cup poured into another makes different waters; tears shed by one eye would blind if wept into another's eye. The breast we strike in joy is not the breast we strike in pain. . . . Rear up, eternal river, here comes grief" (32). The crisis of marginality works itself out in isolation, mis-reading, failed understanding. The margins never take up the center in daylight. The lesbian of Nightwood is arrested on the other side—somnambule by day, renegade wanderer by night. In *Ladies Almanack*, Barnes remarks of her lesbian subjects, those women "born with a Difference" (26), that they "swing between two Conditions like a Bell's Clapper, that can never be said to be anywhere, neither in the Centre, nor to the Side, for that which is always moving, is in no settled State long enough to be either damned or transfigured" (48). Their identities are unsettled, and, thus, unsettling: "The very

Condition of Woman is so subject to Hazard, as complex, and so grievous, that to place her at one Moment is but to displace her at the next" (55). This is doubtless the kind of ontological speculation which captivates readers (writers) like Brossard. The absence of specification leaves the subject, and hence the writing task, open as it propels us on a complex course of speculation.

At first, Barnes seems like one who (before the letter) writes against Lacan, or perhaps she epitomizes Lacan's mirror stage theory through her characters' failures to "identify" themselves.[3] In the moment of the mirror stage, the illusion of identity and the access to language are formed and fused. Barnes experiences the horror in the schizophrenia of the subject and object both being oneself; she produces from/with/in this the crisis of style that is *Nightwood* and lesbianism. Barnes never bought the buoyancy of the illusion (or allusion to wholeness, Identity). Maybe she looked in the mirror and wasn't there. Nora, for example, had "that mirrorless look of polished metals" in her eyes (52). Or perhaps it is that she believed it all too keenly at first, making the dis-illusionment so strong. She faces (up to) the split, head on, eyes open. Perhaps this occasions the terror that Brossard reads in Barnes, the horror I see as a life/style in crisis, *in extremis*, that is, in the shadow of death.

Dear L,

I want to tell Djuna Barnes that she made her life hard. She prepares us for the worst. The lover's heart lays down strata of affections for the lover, prompts a new cartography of love.

In *Nightwood*, the lovers' home becomes a museum, or better, a mausoleum, encrypting life, requiring geologic identification of its fossilized contents. It's a warning to us all. Barnes's work encourages us to vigilance.

We made a promise in our first months together, living in a small apartment and sharing a study. We said we would always remember that where and how we lived didn't matter, that we would never confuse services with affection. We said that we wanted our relationship to be about something else. I think it is.

I hope that we can keep making new fabrics, knitting and unraveling, knitting and unraveling, with the vigilance and persistence of Penelope, because I understand from reading *Nightwood* how crisis enters the interstices.

Still,

L

Critics frequently comment on what Kannenstine referred to as *Nightwood*'s "trans-generic design" (103). Ellen G. Friedman and Miriam Fuchs liken the novel to Woolf's *Orlando*, noting their points of resemblance: "Although its tone and spirit are much darker, *Nightwood* has a number of affinities with Woolf's *Orlando*—its hermaphroditic characters, its basically picaresque movement, its deliberate effort to provide an antigenre" (18–19). There is almost a sense in which these anti-gender novels also result in anti-genre texts, as though, among these lesbian writers, the anti-gender stance demands an anti-genre text. The issue of experimentalism, as Donna Gerstenberger persuasively argues, goes beyond the complex but shared context of the avant-garde. Writers like Stein and Barnes fell into extended periods of critical neglect while Eliot's *The Waste Land* was eagerly adopted by the the New Critics (131). (Carolyn Burke makes a similar point with slightly different players: Barnes and Loy versus Pound and Joyce [Broe, ed., *Silence and Power* 68]). The reason, as Gerstenberger sees it, is that "*Nightwood* demands . . . a reading against the dominant text of binary oppositions by which the Western world inscribes itself." Instead, Barnes rages against traditional verbal and narrative structures, "which create a history built on the oppositions of night/day, past/present, reason/madness, 'normal'/'abnormal,' truth/falsehood, gender, and origins (both historical and textual)" (130). Gerstenberger's provocative analysis, which will certainly help future readers to appreciate Barnes's contribution to experimental writing, disappoints me nonetheless.

To prepare the ground for a poststructuralist reading, Gerstenberger takes issue with Shari Benstock's treatment of Barnes in *Women of the Left Bank*. Her complaint is that Benstock and other recent critics "tend to read the novel in both the cultural and obligatory countercultural terms of Barnes's lesbianism and her biographical misfortunes in love" (131).[4] The challenge is, rather, to get it both ways, to read *Nightwood* in ways compatible with the interests of readers like both Benstock and Gerstenberger. I have to say this, because, predictably, I don't want to write "the lesbian" out of discussions of Barnes in order to preserve either a postmodern theoretical consistency or a pure and positive lesbian identity. But then neither do I want to settle for an easy, binding definition of "the lesbian" in order to make my claims about writing. Barnes is a good subject, if, like me, you want it both ways. She offers a textual radicality that encompasses gender and loss, as she vigorously pursues a (lesbian) anti-romantic aesthetic, demanding, as Gerstenberger correctly notes, "readers for whom contingency and the elaborate alchemy of uncertainty have explanatory power" (137). In my view, Gerstenberger ends her analysis at a point which not only permits but requires the inclusion of lesbianism; she observes in her final paragraph the "probable failure" of *Nightwood*'s "characters to survive a world whose clear message is that 'Thou shalt be one thing or another' within terms of established certainties" (137–38). Barnes's ability to con/found gender, so entrenched in sociocultural fixity, distinguishes her from many experimental writers of her time, while it also points up her similarities to other lesbian experimentalists. Showing itself variously—in what Marcus calls the rupture of the psychoanalytic structure where "the patient asks the questions and the doctor answers" ("Laughing" 233), and in the regendering of God to "she" as O'Connor's act of revenge (150), the critique of gender necessarily requires other tales for the telling.

According to Wittig, Barnes's work "is the first of its kind, and it detonates like a bomb where there has been nothing before it. So it is that, word by word, it has to create its own context, working, laboring with nothing against everything" (66). She continues, "What had there been in literature between

Sappho and Barnes' *Ladies Almanack* and *Nightwood?* Nothing"
(66). The originality of Barnes's *Nightwood* as an experimental
lesbian text is a point worth foregrounding at every turn, even
though those terms—"experimental" and "lesbian"—place rig-
orous demands on us as readers.

Critics frequently discuss the ways in which O'Connor fronts
Barnes's meditation on homosexuality, but they do not always
return to connect their claims to aesthetic matters. In relation to
this first point, Carolyn Allen contends that in *Nightwood* and
some of Barnes's stories, she "explodes" the binarity underlying
Western philosophical thought: "By refusing the categories male
and female, by shifting terms of sexual difference, Barnes' texts
become radical examinations of dichotomous difference. By refusing to take maleness and the phallus as the norm, by questioning the construction of gender and the nature of sexuality, they
rupture the surface of convention and illuminate the world of
night" (55). "Rupture" and "illumination." Something is broken
or exploded, something is lit up for all who care to see. Allen's
terms are quite right, although perhaps this hints at Gerstenberger's objection to "lesbian" readings of the novel; more than "the
surface of convention" is ruptured, and more than "the world of
night" illuminated.

Judith Lee makes a fine contribution to this point in her
consideration of gender and genre. She notes that *Nightwood*
contains four "anti-fairy tales" which deconstruct the opposition
between masculine and feminine because the categories fail to
"define the most fundamental experience of difference: the difference between the identity one imagines (the self as Subject)
and the identity one experiences in relationship with someone
else (the self as Other)" (208). Within this context, I want to
return to my earlier claim that in *Nightwood*, Barnes, through
her critique of gender, constructs an attack on the privileged
aesthetic tradition of much of the nineteenth and twentieth centuries. She rewrites the romance of romanticism, a perspective
best illustrated in O'Connor's discussion of the nature of "this
love we have for the invert, boy or girl" (136). For the heroine

and the hero of heterosexual romance Barnes substitutes the homosexual, remarking on the girl in the boy that makes him a prince, and the lost girl who is the found prince. Barnes goes right to the heart of the romance and appropriates it for her own transformative purposes; thus, all efforts to "save" the princess, in the service of either heterosexual or lesbian romance, fail (Lee 209).

Djuna Barnes is a lesbian I would not want to be. Anaïs Nin, in a letter to Barnes, remarks on the horror Barnes recorded in *Nightwood:* "While I read it I felt: she knows too much, she sees too much, it is intolerable. It was intolerable" (239). The "too much" again, in an/other guise—excess, escaping the bounds of representation. It was not easy to live Barnes's life, to live so long, to be so out of touch, to be so undervalued, to be so exacting about how the world represents you, to renounce yourself. So why should a lesbian read her? Because we suffer crises, we experience "the euphoria and daring of a cultural moment" —the rationale Susan Lanser advances for the celebratory tone of *Ladies Almanack* in the face of "the historical Barnes" (168). Lanser concludes, "Barnes may finally, then, have been articulating a universe less of her own desire than of the desires of those who were at once her friends, readers, and characters. Such a concept challenges notions of the unitary writing subject and traditional images of the nature of writing in relationship to authorial identity" (168). Furthermore, such a breach between the historical Barnes and the textual Barnes might serve as a caution to those of us engaged in codifying a lesbian literary tradition.

Barnes's crisis of style issues from posing the question: how can I write about what lesbian love is? Crisis occurs because the adequacies of representation to answer such a question have been found wanting. As Frann Michel observes, "Barnes's inscriptions of gender and sexuality become more accessible when one notices that Barnes shares with poststructuralist writers on the feminine the assertion that Woman has no single, stable place but rather is multiple, indefinable, outside or beyond ordered systems of representation and thought" (34). Robin Vote, as the enigmatic lesbian subject of *Nightwood,* remains, at the novel's end, even more unsettled as Barnes works at "simultaneously writing and unwriting the practice of representation" (Michel 40). In the novel's remarkable closing section, "The Possessed," readers come closest to the terror of unrepresentability, the "too much" of Djuna Barnes. It becomes clear, in the end, that Robin is not "possessed"—not by Felix, Nora or Jenny, nor by O'Connor's rhetoric, or even by Barnes's narrative; neither is she in possession of her self.[5] She is a beast in the sense that she is unsocialized, undomesticated, willful, a point Benstock makes with respect to Nora's inability to "read" Robin (258). A beast, but no one's pet. Becoming "lesbian," not woman. Such a characterization of Robin leaves the issue of lesbian representation open. What or who is the "real lesbian"? Who can tell her story? She is the one who takes after "Sappho" (136), a blank page of Zeig and Wittig's *Lesbian Peoples: Material for a Dictionary.* Hers is, as the narrator says of Robin, "flesh that will become myth" (37; see Gilbert and Gubar 361), her existence, as "lesbian," a textual one in which the blanks are variously filled in. Only "becoming" lesbian rather than "being" lesbian, written in a grammar terrifying for those, like Nora, who need to know or believe they do.

Dear L,

We are at the end of all romance, resolutely ourselves, flash frames of substituted images, interchangeable but not blurring or merging—thrilling transgressions of those stubborn boundaries that mark one of us off from the other. Even in orgasm, I know you are the one who is giving it to me.

Emptiness accompanies the belief in a failed transcendence. The romantic myth gone awry, shown up more than a century later, for the disaster it has always spelled. I know now that fusion (and transcendence too) is, as the poet says, an exertion that declines. There is a definite pleasure in the fierce separateness our minds insist upon, and I think we are the better for it.

The green wood, the liquid world as lesbian love site (Zimmerman 81–82) never wanted our participation. To (con)script nature as the medium for our love is to subject it once more to the crimes of human nature. Instead, they, the green world and the seas, need only our most gentle and infrequent attention to see that they are allowed to do what they do best. Who, after all, is the guest in this house?

Love,

L

Djuna Barnes is certainly the most elusive figure I will be discussing in this volume. We have recently been given another chance with her. The publication in 1991 of *Silence and Power*, a collection of critical essays edited by Mary Lynn Broe, presents many of the best essays on Barnes previously published in the United States and adds new ones, offering a broader readership another opportunity, the chance of the decade perhaps, to re : find Djuna Barnes. I suspect that, if we can keep her alive among lesbian readers, she will be pursued as relentlessly in her texts as she was in Greenwich Village. I wrote her a letter once, and I know someone who left roses on her doorstep. We were among those lesbians she complained about. But it is as important for us to (re)mark our affections as it was for her to write. Bertha Harris offers the keenest rationale when she says of her own pursuit of Barnes and lesbian literature, "the primary gesture toward the making at last of a decent literature out of the experience of a decent world might simply be a woman like myself following a woman like Djuna Barnes, and all she might represent down a single street on a particular afternoon" (quoted by Stimpson, *Where* 110). Yes, Harris pursued her too. I wonder how many more of us ever tried to follow her down?

FOUR

Gertrude Stein and Me: A Revolution in the Letter

everybody asks me do I know Gertrude Stein, and I always say yes I know her but she is something I keep for myself.

—Avery Hopwood, reported by Stein to Carl Van Vechten

First religion   Alphabets are a way of say
a b c.
Second religion   Alphabets are a way of expressing love for you and for me.
Third religion   Alphabets are in the way.
Fourth religion   Alphabets are as one may say
alphabets today.

—Gertrude Stein, "Lend a Hand or Four Religions"

How to speculate on the debt of another coming back to, amounting to [à soi revenant] oneself?

—Jacques Derrida, The Post Card

Yes, I know Gertrude Stein too. I have known her since the day I knew I was a lesbian. I knew both at once, something about the one connecting the other. That is worth understanding in some detail—a lesbian convergence, and here for the first time I bring them together, literally, in the letter. Ida was the text of my revolutionary summer, which is why I want to say that it signals an affirmation and an upheaval that pushes beyond Orlando, The Well of Loneliness or Nightwood. When I think of lesbian love letters, letters that inscribe lesbian affection, I think of Stein, and especially of Ida, and the summer of 1969.

In a note to the first chapter of his path-breaking work, Hart

Crane and the Homosexual Text, Thomas Yingling makes a comment that epitomizes the difference between Djuna Barnes's crisis and Gertrude Stein's revolution in the letter. Yingling notes that T. S. Eliot "is most insistent that it is discipline and tradition, the sacrifice of self and play, that are the hallmarks of the true artist, and one ought to investigate the meaning of this repression on a personal level and ask as well why this theory gained such acceptance as a cultural truth in Anglo-American letters" (230 fn 17). From childhood, Gertrude Stein never sacrificed anything—neither self nor play. As she observed, she never knew what it meant to "lend a hand": "Can you refuse me can you confuse me can you amuse me can you use me. She said can you. Sweet meat complete tender mender defend her joy alloy and then say that" ("Lend" 186). For this, she has been disliked by the romantic, the politically correct, and the self-sacrificing. Even as insightful and perhaps sympathetic a critic as Catharine Stimpson holds her affection in check; there is something she dislikes about Stein: "She was a genius, whom I honor, but one with several disagreeable traits" ("Mind" 489).[1]

Dear L,

There is a resistance in the letter, in the bridge relating sender and receiver, as tenuous a connection as the one linking this noun and that verb, but still a resistance designed not to yield easily. The body too resists, another set of forces of habit, making us unsuitable for certain work, demanding a wardrobe of its own.

I am defensive about Gertrude Stein, because she is my lesbianism. I think that who likes her would like me too. That doesn't mean that she and I would necessarily agree, about lesbian : writing or lovers, or about politics. But then we don't need to agree. I imagine that when people look at me, and think about it, they remember something of her. I like that, hoping she pleases them. When you look at me, what do you see and remember?

Love,

L

Precisely what bothers Stimpson is difficult to deduce; nor do I believe that she is alone in her resistance. Fifer, for example, refers to Stein's "intricate and elaborate system of self-justification," as she makes herself "the hero of a narcissistic fairy tale," and practices a "simple hedonism" whereby pleasure is maximized and pain minimized (477). (To minimize pain was, I thought, the politically correct feminist gesture: pleasure must be the sticking point.) Stimpson notes in "The Somagrams of Gertrude Stein," "The fact that her work provokes so much ridicule and anxiety—which often masks itself as ridicule—is one mark of her radical-ism" (32). These issues of anxiety and resistance are pressing ones because they might be said to characterize the lesbian and feminist critical evaluation of Stein, one of the greatest modern lesbian writers.[2] Furthermore, such an assessment serves the conventional interests which have kept Stein's work undervalued through the century. I do not mean to suggest that critical judgments should be single (simple)-minded and unqualified; rather, I want to insist that our resistances be probed and our hesitations and convergences made public in the interest of debate.

So what are those "disagreeable traits" in Stein that Stimpson points to and that serve as her cause for reserve in the context of the generous attention she pays? Stimpson observes in "Soma-grams" that Stein, in the first decade of the twentieth century, "was fearful of what she might say, of what she might confess—to herself and others. She disguised her own lesbian experiences by projecting them onto others or by devising what William Gass . . . has called her 'protective language' " (35). These charges, in addition to the suggestion of others—that she suppressed her lesbian texts, *Q.E.D.*, for example, that she was fat, that she enjoyed independent means and took advantage of the attendant privileges, and that she recapitulated a heterosexual male-dominant (Gertrude)/female-submissive (Alice) structure in her personal relationship—make her, in the minds of some, unsuit-able, unattractive, or at least politically incorrect as a lesbian role model.

In this light, the time and circumstance under which Gertrude Stein wrote warrant consideration. Despite Stimpson's evidence on women's education in 1900 ("Mind" 489–90), an 1896 letter to Stein from an older Radcliffe friend, Margaret Sterling Snyder, characterizes the broader milieu within which the writer made her choices: "Will it do you one bit of good as a deterent [to the decision to enter medical school] if I tell you . . . that I now see I was one of the most deluded and pitiable of all these many young women who are aspiring after what is beyond them in our own day. My dear Gertrude, I have no explanations and no theories; I do not know enough to have. But I will say in a word that a sheltered life, domestic tastes, maternity, and faith are all I could ask for myself or you or the great mass of womankind" (*Flowers* 8). Her sister-in-law Sarah Stein offered similar advice the next year: "There certainly is nothing in the line of happiness to compare with that which a mother derives from the contemplation of her first-born and even the agony which she endures from the moment of its birth does not seem to mar it, therefore my dear and beloved sister in law go and get married, for there is nothing in this whole wide world like babies—Leo to the contrary, notwithstanding" (*Flowers* 14). Of course this is only recently outmoded advice, but it replicates that given to me by my master's advisor in 1967, and it reflects an ethos underwriting socio-cultural expectations in the United States to this day.

What is there in the charge that Stein is narcissistic? People frequently describe her that way. I wonder if it is because Toklas cooked, cleaned, and typed for her—performed the domestic tasks other women urged Stein to fulfill herself by doing—or because Stein did what she wanted to do, or called herself a genius and was prickly with friends. Stein still threatens or offends some of her critics, in part because her writing is so willfully itself, refusing the conventions which help readers make sense of texts. People don't like what they don't understand; it's simple. But the real problem with Stein is that unforgivable ego, the very notion that a woman, particularly a lesbian and/or a feminist, should have one—that's what terrifies, isn't it? It locates her beyond/out of control, in a zone feminism assigns to the masculine.

In the twentieth century, "narcissist," like "lesbian" and "homosexual," are clinical words from the psychological lexicon; they construct deviants.

narcissism—1. Excessive admiration of oneself. 2. *Psychoanalysis.* An arresting of development at, or a regression to, the infantile stage of development in which one's own body is the object of erotic interest.

As the logic goes, the lesbian woman must be "narcissistic," loving her own image, because she is in love with "the same," since her love object is not a man; the "not man" is just another woman, lover and lover, woman + woman, the same: she might as well be loving herself. (I have this malady too, but at times I don't think I love myself enough; maybe this is related to the "Stein" in me. Sometimes I'm sure there is no such thing as enough.) But "deviant" or not, the lesbian (in) Stein refuses to go underground. She insists on existing; on being counted—recognition and/or radicality; on her corporeality ("outsized," as Stimpson puts it; *Female* 30), and on her lesbian pleasure. And she likes it. Despite observations to the contrary, Stein insists on going public, to the extent that the public allows her. Here she goes:

From "Idem the Same—A Valentine to Sherwood Anderson" (1923):

If you hear her snore
It is not before you love her
You love her so that to be her beau is very lovely
She is sweetly there and her curly hair is very lovely
She is sweetly here and I am very near and that is very lovely.
She is my tender sweet and her little feet are stretched out well which
    is a treat and very lovely.
Her little tender nose is between her little eyes which close and are
    very lovely.
She is very lovely and mine which is very lovely.

(*Sherwood Anderson/Gertrude Stein* 31).

Here is Stein's real valentine, part of her very fine valentine to Sherwood Anderson, "very fine very mine," but the real valentine sweetheart, the one with sweet feet, a treat to behold, is Toklas, her tender nose recalling the tender buds that form the exergue to this valentine: "In which way are stars brighter than they are. When we have come to this decision. We mention many thousands of buds. And when I close my eyes I see them" (*Anderson/Stein* 31). And again, from *How to Write* (1931): "It is pretty to love a pretty person and to think of her when she is sleeping very pretty" (359). These are bold moves, anticipated in English only to a degree by Whitman and Wilde. After Stein met Toklas in 1907, her life/style changed.

A brief comparative chronology throws Stein's position and accomplishments into relief. Born in 1876, six years before Virginia Woolf and sixteen years before Djuna Barnes, Stein lived almost the first third of her life in the Victorian period; she was 26 when the twentieth century began.[3] Her mother died when she was 14, her father a few years later. Unlike Woolf and Barnes, Stein never married. She wrote *Q.E.D.* (or *Things as They Are*), the story of a lesbian triangle at Radcliffe, in 1903, though she didn't publish it in her lifetime.[4] In 1914 she published *Tender Buttons*, and in 1917 wrote the erotically charged *Lifting Belly*, a book Richard Bridgman finds "luridly" concerned with Stein's private life (149). (Joyce's *Portrait of an Artist* came out in 1916 and *Ulysses* in 1922.)[5] The explicit sustained sexual pleasure of Stein's life/style is definitely more evident in the texts collected in the *Yale Edition of the Unpublished Writings of Gertrude Stein*, where works like "Bee Time Vine" and *Lifting Belly* display little ambiguity, although they are not necessarily easier to read:

> Kiss my lips. She did.
> Kiss my lips again she did.
> Kiss my lips over and over and over again she did.
> (*Lifting* 20)

But even in these texts, what strikes us as ambiguous or oblique —"lifting belly," for example—might be seen as an effort to construct rather than to mask a lesbian (sem)eroticism.

In the context of Stein's lesbianism, the work of Cynthia Secor, one of her earliest and best critics, has received noticeably less attention than it deserves. In her 1979 paper on whether or not Stein might be called a "non-declared lesbian," Secor takes a rather different position, the primary points of which are that Stein "was not precisely one to dodge lesbian and feminist issues" (1); that she wrote, preserved and shared with friends her overtly sexual and lesbian works (2)—"They were written to be read" (13); that, had she published these works, they, like *Ulysses*, would have been promptly banned (2);[6] that it was appropriate for *Q.E.D.*, as juvenilia, to remain unpublished. To my mind, these are persuasive arguments that, curiously, are not reprinted in either of the two recent collections (those edited by Hoffman and Bloom) of Stein criticism.

The most striking and controversial points Secor makes— ones not listed above, because they are not really part of the "mainstream"/feminist controversy about Stein, are the following observations: (1) had Stein's lesbian writings been published, they would have had "far less chance [than Joyce's] of being understood and championed by the predominately male literary establishment" (2); (2) Stein is among the first writers since Sappho to write about lesbian sexual experience; (3) Stein's interest in rhythm reflects her lesbianism: "Without the patriarchal conventions of marriage, it is rhythm, finely tuned and retuned over the years, that holds individuals together. Furthermore, the sexuality of two women at its best is rhythm as fine tuned as it is ever likely to be experienced" (6). These must be, by some standards, indecorous observations, ones not worth reprinting a decade later, yet they seem to me to be among the most trenchant feminist observations produced by any of her critics on the subject of lesbian : writing and Gertrude Stein. They suggest what a lesbian : writing today finds there and why it is important to look.

True, I don't need to be convinced. I love Gertrude Stein because she refuses to hide, and she puts herself first: "she passes and passes and she surpasses" ("Lend" 177); "She is here and perfection" ("Lend" 182). "Here" is not here, in the presence of company, but here in the present moment of reader and text, of letter and page—the only present that a reader as reader can ever know. Gone before you know it.

Dear L,

I could, à la Gertrude Stein, give you/us many names, or the same name, L and L. Stein created her women in pairs, in twins, Ida-Ida: "There were two, she and she were there" (*Two* 135).[7] Or more: Ida, Ida-Ida, Winnie, or even Winnie Winnie. Lesbians who live together are often taken as sisters, "twins" of a sort. In every out of the way stopping place, the kind where cashiers and waitresses expect to talk to you, they ask: are you two sisters? But we've caught on now. They've asked each of us the same question with other lovers. People try to construct an acceptable relationship to connect two unrelated women, especially women who look "that way," the way we do. But Stein also knew, as the title of one of her pieces—"Three Sisters Who Are Not Sisters"—suggests: these sisters are not sisters.

Longing for my lovely twin,

L (& L)

Ida, like many of Stein's texts, could be called a valentine, a love letter. Stimpson describes it as a "rhetoric . . . of love. For she saw naming as an act of love—done for love, with love, in love. What, in brief, we do for love" ("Transposition" 8).[8] Stimpson characteristically, however, undercuts this observation in her very next sentence where she claims that Stein "is the woman writer only partly freed from patriarchal ideologies of work and love, her rhetoric is that of the conventional male role in a love affair: desire; command; fear of rejection; gratification; and abandonment" (8). This argument hinges on the notion that the language of love as desire, fear, control and gratification is, for Stein, a masculine language. In fact, I cannot imagine any masculine parallels in the fiction of the period. These subjects and their treatment are no one's private property. If anything, this rhetoric of love, as spoken by Stein, a lesbian, marks her revolutionary relationship with Alice Toklas in writing. Judy Grahn explains that Stein challenges "our very basic patterns of relationship, at the level of linguistic relationship" (11): "life" and "style" are inseparable. With Alice Toklas, Gertrude Stein's life/style splits open, the difference, for example, between or within the lesbian texts, *Q.E.D.* and *Lifting Belly*.

Similarly, the multiplied excitement of *Ida* issues from its opening paragraph, begins with Ida's birth—the birth of the character, the first letters of the novel, the birth of the lesbian subject: "There was a baby born named Ida. Its mother held it with her hands to keep Ida from being born but when the time came Ida came. And as Ida came, with her came her twin, so there she was Ida-Ida" (7). In her correspondence, Stein explains that the birth of *Ida*, the book, was difficult and slow, as though she were aware that the time needed to be right.

In the beginning, Ida, sitting with her blind dog Love, writes letters to her twin.

Dear Ida my twin,
    Here I am writing not alone because I have dear Love with me, and I speak to him and he speaks to me, but here I am all alone and I am thinking of you Ida my dear twin. Are you beautiful as I am dear twin Ida, are you. . . . but you dear Ida you are not, you are not here, if you were I could not write to you. Do you know what I think Ida, I think that you could be a queen of beauty. . . . Dear Ida oh dear Ida do do be one. Do not let them know you have any name but Ida and I know Ida will win, Ida Ida Ida,
                                          from your twin
                                          Ida. (19)

Three such letters appear in the opening pages of the novel, the third addressed to Winnie, the name Ida(-Ida) in the second letter threatens to call her twin Ida, and a notion anticipated in the first letter. Chessman explains this well: "The letter acts as the bond between Ida and Ida, the longer, linguistic manifestation of the copula [as "a visual mark" of a "potentially erotic link" (179)] between the two Idas in the book's opening" (178). But thereafter, with the proliferation of subjects, the twinning of characters, animals, and places, we could say that all letters are letters. How is it, after all, that one (character) becomes two, or more: one letter follows another.

What is Stein's position with respect to a lesbian subject(ivity)? Is she simply a "woman" playing a "man," assuming "masculine authority in her private life" (Benstock 184)—another father, another Leo? Is she the "husband" and Toklas the "Mrs.," as Stimpson suggests and which Benstock extends to a relationship with "sadomasochistic elements" (165)? It is far from the misguided version of heterosexual "marriage" that critics like Stimpson and Benstock allege it is. We can say that Stein had a "wife" in Alice, the typist, cook and companion, only if we mean by that no more than a set of relational functions, an array of tasks with differing relations to the private and the public sector. Women, after all, do not have "wives"; their lovers are not women in/of the heterosex(t)ual economy.[9] Stein and Toklas are not "the same" and seem as a result to violate some fundamental feminist taboo concerning equality. (Therefore this must be a "marriage," and Stein must be the "husband." It's funny that she never sounds or looks like one to me.)

Joan Nestle's comments about the lesbian/feminist community's embarrassment when confronted with butch-femme lesbians' public signification of "women's erotic autonomy" (*Restricted* 102) explain in part the impetus behind reactions to Stein (notice too that it is Stein, that butchy dyke, who is always to blame). Nestle's caution bears repeating here: "Butch-femme relationships, as I experienced them, were complex erotic statements, not phony heterosexual replicas" (100). Lesbian : readings of Stein as "the butch" tend to look at her suspiciously, discussing her as the male partner (enemy) whom lesbianism tries to avoid and dismissing the "masculine" as a structural position even though some lesbians might strive to attain it. As Judith Roof points out in her superb analysis (*Lure* 244–45), butch/femme is regarded, in the most benign terms, as a failure of lesbian imagination that merely superimposes "a male/female model on lesbian relations," whereas "Butch/Femme, however, is internally self-contradictory from the beginning" (245).

Even Benstock, despite her insistence on heterosexual terminology, hints at this complexity in Stein's roles—"she was husband to Alice, the baby their marriage had produced, and the Mother of Us All" (193). And what about the "Baby Woojums" Stein played to Toklas's "Mama Woojums" and Carl Van Vechten's "Papa Woojums"? And the letters to their friend "Kiddy" (W. G. Rogers)? Then the "sisters" too. These designations, which appear throughout Stein's letters, derive from family constellations, but the endless substitutability of roles and players suggests an arrangement far different from the heterosexual nuclear family which takes its name from the father. In his discussion of *Tender Buttons*, Neil Schmitz observes: "A 'sister' appears in the text, sharing the ambiguity of the writer's *that*, like and unlike, whose cookery and cleaning, whose intimacy is woven into the intellectual and imaginative work of the writer. . . . 'The sister was not a mister'. . . . She is for the writer the positive identification of a likeness, a part of *that*, the sister self, the daughter self, a reflection, and in *Tender Buttons* (tend her buttons) she is positively cherished" (164). The blurring of subject and object, or subject in object and vice versa, confounds the conventional task and role polarities that historically determine our ability to differentiate between male and female. Certainly, the point of "the sister was not a mister" is the absence of all misters from this tale of domestic relations. At the same time, Harriet Chessman observes with respect to *Ida*, the subject depends upon the object's difference: "Ida 'comes' because another (an 'other') comes 'with her': the two Idas represent, in this sense, self and other, in that an identity comes into existence only through the presence of difference. Rather than a Lacanian loss of a narcissistic and fictive wholeness and unitariness, however, this achievement of identity through difference appears to represent a gain and an addition: Ida *and* Ida" (168–69). We might read the difference between Barnes and Stein as a difference Lacan's mirror stage illuminates, where Barnes focuses in *Nightwood* on the horror of loss through fracturing the "unified self," Stein suggests the playful dimension of endless multiplication in *Ida*.

Stein's revolution in the letter confounds as much as it reproduces the discourse of heterosexuality. Thus, Schmitz concludes his consideration of the plays on Ada, aider, alas, Alice, by noting, "The text [of *Tender Buttons*] resounds with the exchanges of these two figures, lover/beloved, writer/speaker, both of whom mirror each other. Lovetalk is double-talk, *ma jolie*, and the lovetalk of wedded lesbians is doubled double-talk, turned against the espionage of the straight world" (167). The doubled double talking of the twinned Ida-Ida, of the writer and her aider, alas/alias/Alice, of the lesbian lover and her lov(h)er[10] represent moves more radically unsettling in the (con)text of a gendered discourse than the simple substitution of a homosexual "same" for a heterosexual "different."

Dear Lovey,

There you are in the next room, so far away you might as well be in Key West. So I miss you and want to write to you. Didn't we begin by/in writing, our first meeting a letter?

These letters sometimes contain private jokes that only you will recognize. This one in itself is also a reference to the letters surrounding it. (Don't overlook or omit it.) Others may understand what I mean. They might not like it, but then again, some might.

Love,

L

Stein could not have given us her lesbian : writing without Alice B. Toklas—not because of the feeding, tending, and typing, but because of loving her, constructing her as the site of composition, epitomized in the grand joke that is *The Autobiography of Alice B. Toklas*, but as well in the playful energy of her style. She writes her love(r). Schmitz elaborates:

She [Alice] is effectively the framing language of the domocile, a feminine speech distributed among its traditional concerns—household objects, food, rooms—and therein a response to the question in Gertrude Stein's mind about relation and resemblance. So Alice B. Toklas is in *Tender Buttons*, not as an autobiographical reference, not as a specific character, but as the very space in which the writing (and the question) of *Tender Buttons* takes place, as the tender and the button. (174)

While Stein's relationship with Toklas is implicitly inscribed in the autobiographies, the unpublished works, and in "Ada," in *Ida* it represents another instance of Stein's revolution of style in life and letters.

One can argue, as Stacy Hubbard does, that Stein worries in these and other texts, including *Ida,* about identity, which, for a moment frees itself from heterosexual gender divisions. Hubbard cleverly proposes alternative titles for *Ida: "The Novel (i.e., new) Autobiography of I-I-I-Ida,* or *The Life History of a Personified Pronoun"* (3). Observing the sliding gender in the pronoun references, and the twinning of Andrew as well as Ida, Hubbard comments: "Ida is more than an 'I' . . . she is a 'he' and a 'she' and an 'it,' she is an 'I' plus an 'And,' a pronoun conjoined (conjugally) to a conjunction: I (Ida) and-you (Andrew). Together they utter the stutter of love, and Ida begins, like the genius she is, to rest and do nothing, nothing at all" (10). Furthermore, the "I" of Ida, just like the "first" of Andrew the first, represents the theme of pronoun reference and identity, or how (pro)nouns (mis)represent identity. Hubbard argues that "Andrew is said to be 'Andrew the first' or what we might call 'the first person,' that is, the perfect echo of Ida's 'I.' Moreover, Andrew is said to be 'a sign' because 'the first of anything is [always] a sign' (119)" (10).

I/da I/da Ida. What is the "da" of I/da? It recalls that other "da" from the *fort/da* game, of the pleasure principle at work, materializing itself in the letter. *Ida* offers an oblique commentary on the *fort/da* game that Freud recounts in *Beyond the Pleasure Principle* (see Chessman 170). His grandson plays a game expressive of his alienation, as he tosses his toy out of sight (*fort*, away/gone) like his mother, and recovers it, actually materializes it (*da*, there) at will (8–11). Stein's "continuous present" becomes a style—rather like Lacan's "relation of desire to desire" in which alienation represents itself—that permits the ongoingness of pleasure, as absence (*fort*) necessarily expresses itself through presence (*da*), the extension of bliss-in-Alice.[11] No punctuation to interrupt this. But Stein gives us more than the constant recuperation of psychic balance; she writes a form of ecstasy, Derrida's definition of which serves well here: "Ecstasy: to relive the first time better than the first time, and first of all to anticipate this in the void of the first of the first times, *and so on*" (*Post Card* 228). The life/style insists—representing, repeating, substituting—as it seeks a sexual/textual economy based on the "better than the first time" that is not (the void). Lesbian (sem)erotics: an ecstasy at work.

Ida expresses her difference from herself by writing her twin. Stein writes her twin Ida who writes Winnie: "Sure I know Winnie. Everybody knows who Winnie is" (24). Ida overhears some people in a shoe store talking about Winnie, a man comes to her house and asks for Winnie, who is not Ida (the I having *fort*, "Stein" the "writer" not there, but in the text, the caller only able to recognize "I"-*da*). Ida tells an army officer that "better than anything else . . . I like being where I am. Oh said he excitedly, and where are you. I am not here, she said. I am very careful about that. No I am not here, she said, it is very pleasant, she added and she turned slightly away, very pleasant indeed not to be here" (29). It is "Ida" (or "Stein"), not Ida, who is being addressed, called upon (understood or read):

He asked for Winnie.
Of course there was no Winnie.
That was not surprising
    and did not surprise him
He could not ask for Ida because he did not know Ida. He almost asked
    for Ida. Well in a way he did ask for Ida. (26)

Stein is writing about the experience of identity (like the *fort/da*
as alienation), particularly, in the adulthood that follows the
deaths of one's parents, and after fame, how the self is called
into question when others "know" you. Lesbianism is difficult to
hide from this sort of scrutiny (everyone thinks he or she knows
your secret). But the secret resides elsewhere.

Dear L,
    As I sat in my study, I remembered us on the pier in Santa
Cruz, eating clams out of paper dishes, how later our love was
triangulated as we watched the body of a grey whale rise up full
length out of the surf at Big Sur, and how in Traverse City we
watched the monitors outside the room where they stopped my
mother's heart. You were there. I was there.
    What could the *fort/da* game of adulthood amount to when
we go and return together? What remains when your father is
dead and your mother's heart stops? Perhaps our tenuous hope
of finding new players and new forms that brings us to write
these letters. Are you really the "you" to whom I address my
love? Are you ever "you"? Or "I" I? And are we the ones fucking
in the damp fecund heat of an Alabama afternoon or in the starry
dark azure night on the beach at Gulf Shores?
                                    Stuttering my love for you,
                                                            L

If Stein played the male role, the butch, still she was not a
man, not a "husband" or a "male writer" (or she might have been
taken more seriously); rather, she exemplifies what Nestle re-

gards as the contradictoriness of "butch" and "femme," the way in which they refuse analogy to the heterosexual gender roles of masculine and feminine.[12] In this sense, Stein's life/style lends credence to Wittig's claim that the lesbian is outside the sex-gender system. Perhaps like Stein, Ida (who has many husbands who fail to determine her) finds it "natural" to say yes, she always said yes (even when "you" said no) (138–39),[13] and the "natural" is different, and because it is, it is difficult: "It is not easy to lead a different life, much of it never happens but when it does it is different" (139). Patriarchal binarity fails to account for the lesbian. Thus, Nestle observes of the butch lesbian in the fifties who wore men's clothes, "[she] was not a man wearing men's clothes; she was a woman who created an original style to signal to other women what she was capable of doing—taking erotic responsibility" ("Fem" 235). As Penelope Engelbrecht elaborates, "Because the lesbian cannot occupy either the Subjective or Objective pole of the theoretical binary without provoking contradictions, she must occupy a position 'outside' or marginal to the patriarchal polarity. Naturally, to be 'outside' everything that is, is to be nonexistent. But lesbians exist. Clearly, current Subjective theory simply cannot account for 'lesbian' material reality, which is the basis for lesbian textuality" (89–90). Despite all that has been written about how Stein obscures and encodes her lesbianism, I believe that she insists upon it, that it "insists" in her life and work. Make no mistake: she asserts her erotic responsibility.

By recognizing and resisting the personal crisis of the lesbian in society in favor of affirming sexual differences, Stein offers us, instead, what Barthes calls a "text of bliss," the characterizing feature of which is another kind of crisis in language: "Text of pleasure: the text that contents, fills, grants euphoria, the text that comes from culture and does not break with it, is linked to a *comfortable* reading. Text of bliss: the text that imposes a state of loss, the text that discomforts (perhaps to the point of a certain boredom), unsettles the reader's historical, cultural, psychological assumptions, the consistency of [her or] his tastes, values, memories, brings to a crisis [her or] his relation with language" (*Pleasure* 14).[14] As many critics attest, reading Stein is *not* a "pleasure," the comfortable experience of being at home (with "oneself"), and linked to the tradition of canonical literature. She killed the nineteenth century—"the nineteenth century is dead dead dead" (*Wars* 21)—to tell her/our story. She elected to be an outlaw, to escape her homeland, to read and write English in the midst of France, to love Alice B. Toklas. Knowing that the only safe "outlaw"—sexual or aesthetic—is a dead one, she couples that view with a critique of the "natural," the standard for the law abiding: "Nature is not natural and that is natural enough" (*Ida* 141). She persistently installs herself in the transgressor's (non)place: "the creator of the new composition in the arts is an outlaw until he is a classic, there is hardly a moment in between" (*What* 27). An excitement of disarray and confusion characterizes her work as she stages the breaks from which we can trace an/other past that allows us to construct alternative sexual and artistic trajectories for today. The project's energy emerges in palpable rhythm, syntax, and tonal color: "In the midst of writing there is merriment," she exclaims at the end of *Lifting Belly* (62). Lesbian : writing takes (a) place.

Repetition, assonance, the absence of punctuation, all emphasize the ways in which a text performs the ongoingness of representation (of writing as performance). A vertiginous instability of non-sense sheers off, goes blissing across the page in the ecstasy of Stein's life/style. Concerning autobiography, this story of love and writing that Stein tells herself about herself, Derrida observes in another context: "And since life is on the line, the trait that relates the logical to the graphical must also be working between the biological and the biographical, the thanatological and the thantographical" (*Ear* 4–5). The lesbian body (the biological) writes itself (auto/graphics). Stein the auto-grapher signs her texts.

Dear L,

When I think of you in the next room writing, I imagine what you say is addressed to me. I take every word and am greedy for more. Imagine how Toklas felt, reading the portrait of Ada, knowing it was (written for) her. What did she feel when she read these words: "Trembling was all living, living was all loving, some one was then the other one. Certainly this one was loving this Ada then. And certainly Ada all her living then was happier in living than any one else who ever could, who was, who is, who ever will be living" (*Geography and Plays* 16).

Do you think, as she held the paper, her hand shook? Did she blush? Did Pussy's pussy grow moist and did she close her eyes and moan, just a little? Here I am, almost a century later, wishing I had written this first, and for you, or that tomorrow, when I awaken and go downstairs, I find that you are the one who has left these words for me. A letter on the breakfast table.

Love,

L

In what I view as a lifelong meditation on lesbian : writing, Gertrude Stein devotes herself to evading questions and answers as she keeps the issue of lesbian identity open. Indeed, she avoids the very question itself, but certainly not out of timidity or a desire for recognition. Rather, she adopts a relationship to the wor(l)d that resists the very structure of question/answer (haven't we always known what a tightly intricated pair those are, the heart of the Socratic method, that cornerstone of Western rationality). In *Everybody's Autobiography*, the narrator comments, "To me when a thing is really interesting it is when there is no question and no answer, if there is then already the subject is not interesting and it is so, that is the reason that anything for which there is a solution is not interesting, that is the trouble with governments and Utopias and teaching, the things not that can be learnt but that can be taught are not interesting" (213). When lesbian identity remains open, it remains interesting. A multitude of expressions as well as ways of responding is permitted, much "can be learnt," by one individual over a lifetime and from different individuals living in different moments and circumstances.

Stein's expression of identity, reiterated like a signature—"I am I because my little dog knows me" (64)—reveals this principle at work. The statement replays the pronoun game of I/da: the "I," the subject of the sentence, requires the little dog (Stein had a poodle, for example, named Basket, who, when he died, became Basket I because Basket II took his place), or someone in the little dog's position (a lover, whose names don't really matter—Andrew/Ada/Alice/Pussy, aid/[h]er), to secure the subject position for the speaker. Stein writes in *Ida:* "And now Ida was not only Ida she was Andrew's Ida and being Andrew's Ida was more that Ida she was Ida itself" (90). Stein has been returning to Ida throughout her work—the early portrait "Ida" (1937), the character Ida in *Doctor Faustus Lights the Lights* (1938), and *Ida, A Novel* (1941). She claimed from the beginning "Everybody is an Ida" ("Ida" 46), and in an important way, in the sense of I/da of the *fort/da* game, Stein is certainly right about how she and we are (carried back to) Ida. Identity is a relational and thus changeable effect, or as Derrida remarks: "The ear of the other says me to me and constitutes the autos of my autobiography" (*Ear* 51). Since identity is not fixed, it remains the subject of/in Stein's writing and contemplation: "Identity always worries me and memory and eternity" (*Autobiography* 115).

Insistence keeps the thing before us; it is the acting out of Stein's "worries" about her subject position. Unlike literal repetition, insistence is continuing with a difference, like the frames in cinema—no two moments are alike in a *moving* picture. As Stein observes in *Everybody's Autobiography*, "Having done anything you naturally want to do it again and if you do it again then you know you are doing it again and it is not interesting" (28). Stein's insistence on personal freedom fueled her life/style and reinforced the need for alternatives to the nineteenth century's sexual/textual legacy. In *Wars I Have Seen*, she writes:

"The one thing that everybody wants is to be free, to talk to eat to drink to walk to think, to please, to wish, and to do it now if now is what they want, . . . they do not want to feel imprisoned they want to feel free . . . let the future take care of itself all they want is to be free, not managed, threatened, directed, restrained, obliged, fearful, administered" (75). The lexicon might have founded the terms of Foucault's exposé of the power/knowledge nexus at the heart of institutional sexual regulation: "the word discipline, and forbidden and investigated and imprisoned brings horror and fear into all hearts . . . not to be watched, controlled, and scared, no no, not" (*Wars* 75). While the specific textual reference for these words is World War I, written in light of the experience of World War II, their power is reinforced by a history of textual and sexual regulation—the laws that make outlaws of us.

Again and again, Gertrude Stein wrote lesbian auto-bio-graphy, the life, *bio-*, in writing, *graphy*. Conceived as such, *Everybody's Autobiography* seems all the more radical—most obviously in its subversion of the notion that autobiography is only for the famous rather than everybody, and also in the sense in which, as *lesbian* autobiography, it locates everybody along a lesbian continuum like the one Rich describes decades later. Reading a lesbian : writing puts the reader in relation to a lesbian, con/scripts the reader in(to) a lesbian plot. Specifically, Stein writes us into a grammar of lesbian eroticism. In *How to Write*, she remarks, "I am a grammarian. . . . I love my love with a b because she is precious. I love her with a c because she is all mine" (105). This is an extraordinary grammar—beginning with the absent alpha of this lesbian alpha-bet—[a] = Alice/all mine; b = be-cause she is the precious A. B., and c = be-cause she is Toklas/all mine. Stein's lexical erotics plays both sides of Barthes's pleasure principle: "The word can be erotic on two opposing conditions, both excessive: if it is extravagantly repeated, or on the contrary, if it is unexpected, succulent in its newness (in certain texts, words *glisten*, they are distracting, incongruous apparitions)" (*Pleasure* 42).

So, yes, as I said at the opening of this chapter, I know Gertrude Stein in a way that takes after how she knows herself. She acquires different features as my relationship to her changes. Her letters spark and glisten, move and turn, and I imagine that she wrote them for me. I have always liked Gertrude Stein: she sends me back to myself.

FIVE

Lesbian (Sem)Erotics

The text you write must prove to me *that it desires me*. This proof exists: it is writing. Writing is: the science of the various blisses of language, its Kama Sutra (this science has but one treatise: writing itself).

—Roland Barthes, *The Pleasure of the Text*

If the problem of the Don Juan myth is in fact the problem of the relation of the erotic and the linguistic, the scandal lies not so much in the fact that the linguistic is always erotic, but in the much more scandalous fact that the erotic is always linguistic.

—Shoshana Felman, *The Literary Speech Act*

If jouissance is "beyond the pleasure principle," it is not because it is beyond pleasure but because it is beyond principle.

—Jane Gallop, *Thinking Through the Body*

How is it that lesbian : writing speaks (our) textual/sexual pleasure to us? What are the sources of our enjoyment, the "more than" intellectual pleasure, the perverse pleasure, to which Jane Gallop refers in the following passage: "Textual pleasure is not only perverse sexually (by not serving reproduction of the species), but also without any higher function such as instruction, communication, or ideological stance. Or rather, I would say, it is not that the latter functions do not obtain, but that the pleasure of the text is not subordinate to them in any predictable way" (106). Taken in a lesbian context, I find an interesting coincidence at work here: the converging "perversity" of lesbian sexual/textual pleasure.

Perhaps the very unpredictability—how it stands "outside"

the law—of the ways pleasure presents itself creates pleasure, its construction of the moment or its coming by surprise an essential part of its creation. A circularity inhabits this proposition, as is always the case with the inside and the outside, the frame and the thing framed, the gaze and its object, language and "the real." Gallop calls this "the erotic paradox"—"what I put there is already there"—which she elaborates as follows:

> In order to be erotic, the object must depend on the viewer, on the aroused one, on our fantasies, our imagination, our constructs, our framing, and yet, the object must also remain independent, still real, still other. Eroticism itself is a relation to something that is very much part of our imagination, our projection, our desires. Our eroticism is what is most narcissistic or most imperialistic in our relation to the world, and yet, there is also some relation between our desires and something that is really out there, that is independent of our fantasies. (157)

My desire, in other words, separates "me" from "you." You must be "there" for me to desire "you." The desire is always already in me/you. I see you. My senses construct my love for you as they express (it to) you. I see (parallax) you. When I look at my lesbian lover, I see (my) love. I write a love letter, L, Dear L, V and V, that creates as it inscribes (y/our) love, lover and lover, beloved and beloved.

Dear L,

I want you to look at me, your eyes moving to the dark places like your tongue, but in a crowded room. Your gaze constructs me, holds me as your lover, in an intimacy that knows no peripheral vision; no hindsight either. Your eyes hold me; they work like hands, touching the shell and caressing my pink clit until it begs. You unbutton my jeans, strip off my pants and take me in.

I want you to look at me, take me in your eyes like that, holding me there until nothing exists outside the frame we make, no outside, no before or after, you. Just duration, being enacted there, going on and on and on as we make love together.

Look at me again. I'm ready.

Love,
L

Who speaks this text of seduction? I can write it without you, but not without "you." Can there be a schizophrenia of desire in which I play both parts (woman and woman, lover and beloved) —I invent "you" so that you can take me, I can have you, like Virginia had Vita, at least in writing? The ambiguity masks my ability to know if this desire is your text or mine, if it is the sex of textuality or the text of sexuality. Exploring the relationship between language and action in *The Literary Speech Act*, Shoshana Felman begins by asking, "To speak an act: can this be done? Is it possible to speak seduction—the always scandalous intervention of love in theory, of pleasure in knowledge?" (12). Felman invokes and then departs from Austin's distinction between constative and performative speech acts, where *constatives* are "descriptive utterances . . . sentences that set forth *statements* of fact, that report a state of affairs, true or false," and *performatives*, "expressions whose function is not to inform or to describe, but to carry out a 'performance,' to accomplish an *act* through the very process of their enunciation" (15). In such articulations as "I promise," "I swear," "I apologize," the speaker is accomplishing rather than describing an act, producing the event or action, and thus enacting or performing "operations [which, as such] cannot be logically true or false, but only successful or unsuccessful, 'felicitous' or 'infelicitous' " (16). "I desire" might be one. Word and deed, fact and event, are synonymous, one makes the other.[1]

When I say "I love you," I want my words to perform their function, to turn you on, to recall desire (again). When I write "I love you," I perform my passion in the letter. "I want you": the letters materialize my desire, however imperfectly, mis-guidedly. They stand (in) for anticipation or longing, the absence of what I think I want. These words are as close as I can get to the truth of fact; I ask them to enact my passion. What is the difference, the one without the other?

(Sem)erotics concerns the physical appreciation or response to the textual, when the sexual and the textual fuse in synonymy —what Susie Bright calls "one-handed reading" (86). How does the lesbian viewer/reader (inter)penetrate the scene/seen? How does a text become a physical/sexual event? According to Felman, sex epitomizes the radicality of the convergence of constative and performative: "The human sexual act always connotes the speech act—the act *par excellence* of the speaking body, which subsists only insofar as it speaks, and which cannot know whether it, or the fire that it carries, is after all really a 'thing' or only an 'event' " (111). The line of demarcation where one ends and the other begins blurs. The lesbian body speaks, I hope felicitously, musically, successfully: I love you. It performs an intimacy that I want to remain memorable.

Intimate—1. marked by close acquaintance, association, or familiarity. 2. Pertaining to or indicative of one's deepest nature. 3. Essential; innermost. 4. Characterized by informality and privacy: *an intimate nightclub.* 5. Very personal; private; secret. —See synonyms at *familiar.* —n.

Through the word "intimacy," the most private becomes public, participates in the socio-symbolic system. When I write, I display my intimacy with the letter, not its referent—the word "love(r)," not my love(r) whose shadow inhabits the form, whose shape and feel the letter recalls. This split affords the condition for seduction, which as Felman points out, relies on *separation,* not binding, a leading away from as much as to: "Separation is an *essential* aspect of seduction" (43). As Felman explains, to "make advances" means to engage a spatial structure expressive of "the very tension of the opposition—but also as the vanishing point, even as the incessant displacement—between *behind* and *before,* in back and in front" (47). The word and the "thing,"

held apart textually, creating the (sem)erotic field. A separation :
an ecstasy.

Dear L,

What is the reality of love for you as I write it in words, as the
words say it—love you me. The question I ask repeatedly: What
is/was love before the letter? How to couple them, words and
letters, conjoin them, make them rub up against each other—
my cheek and yours, my leg wrapped around yours. What is the
intimacy of the letter? What happens when one letter touches
another? A blurring and a confusion? Make no mistake what it
means: your fingers in my mouth, this is not a matter of words
my tongue speaks, sliding around those rounded smooth fingers,
the subtle implements of your love.

Loving you,

L

Lesbian sexual/textual pleasure exceeds the effects of representational content. Gallop claims that, generally speaking, all
such pleasure issues from an encounter, "the erotics of engagement": "Subject matter is sexual not because it is *about* some
experience of sexuality, but because we experience the relation
to subject matter in art as forbidden, powerful, desiring, and
embarrassing" (138). Difference locates itself relationally: we
engage the subject matter, as object, in a particular way. In the
particularity of that relationship, transgressing the difference
between subject and object, woman and woman, I want to install
the word "lesbian." Something happens when one woman desires another. Something happens when a woman reads or writes.
As Nicole Brossard puts it, "If I desire a woman, if a woman
desires me, then there is the beginning of writing" (*Aerial* 43).
Certainly there is the beginning of narrative, whether one is a
writer or not. The trajectory of the narrative of consummation
begins there, in the moment of desire. I write our story, in my
mind if not on paper. How I will have her, and, always, how she
will take me.

Brossard excels in the articulation of a lesbian (sem)erotics. In determined moves away from traditional strategies of representation, language and textuality, Brossard's works provide the field within which a lesbian eroticism is figured. The following lines from *Lovhers* demonstrates my point:

> memory, some words are such
> that an embrace conceives
> their surfaces/allusions
> because my obsession with reading
> (with mouths) urges me
> toward every discourse. (39)

The textual/sexual bodies of writer, narrator, critic and lover merge in the line where language is the meeting place of mind and body, sense and sense. On the one hand, word as words are eroticized. On the other, erotic signifiers are figured linguistically. My mouth kisses my lover and speaks to her.

No part of the lesbian body escapes the eroticization of its surface, a million points of access to sensation and arousal. A passage from Brossard's *Picture Theory* illustrates the vertical/spatial working out of erotic energy:

SKIN utopia slow vertigo. I work in the context of our body fluorescence already written. I perform the rites and the temptation of certitude in order that it branch out. I see formal woman opening onto sense for I know that each image of woman is vital in the thinking organism— gyno-cortex. At the end of the patriarchal night, the body foresees itself in the horizon before me on a skin screen, mine, where resonance endures in that which weaves the web *the light* when beneath my tongue ripples the world's reason. M.V. was saying yes. In her eyes it was epidermal, this desire for the aerial circulation of spatial gestures initiated by the letter *Skin*. (*Aerial* 131)

A multidimensional textual/sexual force issues from the convergence of tropes: the astronomical, the linguistic, the cinematic, the physiological. Yes, this must be a "sextual" physiology of lesbian desire. As I catalogue my lover's body—fingers, hands, feet, eyes, nose, knees—every aspect takes on its erotic possibilities. The words can't escape their histories, their futures, ours. I say: any lesbian who is thinking is inventing her (our) future.

The most erotic lesbian text I know is Brossard's "Sous La Langue/Under Tongue," from beginning to end. I could select any of its seven stanzas to demonstrate the production of erotic effect. In order to convey its movement, I quote the third stanza:

You cannot foresee so suddenly leaning toward a face and wanting to lick the soul's whole body till the gaze sparks with furies and yieldings. You cannot foresee the body's being swept into the infinity of curves, of pulsings, every time the body surges you cannot see the image, the hand touching the nape of the neck, the tongue parting the hairs, the knees trembling, the arms from such desire encircling the body like a universe. Desire is all you see. You cannot foresee the image, the burst of laughter, the screams and the tears. The image is trembling, mute polyphonic. Does she frictional she fluvial she essential does she all along her body love the bite, the sound waves, does she love the state of the world in the blaze of flesh to flesh as seconds flow by silken salty cyprin. (182)

As is often the case with Brossard's texts, the passage performs its erotic work on several levels. Some of the words and phrases derive clearly from a language of sexual intercourse: "lick," "furies and yieldings," "tongue parting the hairs," "the bite," "blaze of flesh to flesh," "silken salty cyprin" (glossed as female sexual secretions). This discourse is reinforced by descriptions of the body and its responses: "knees trembling," encircling arms, "the screams and the tears." The stanza itself is made to tremble, pulsating with a texual as well as a sexual desire for consummation: arousal, satisfaction and release. More difficult to derive is the poem's insistence on the complicity of textuality itself. It is an image that moves the lover, a word or perhaps a whole sentence that arouses her. The image, like the knees, is said to tremble. Brossard's text makes palpable Felman's point concerning the referential (in)capacity of language which, she says, is not "a *statement* of the real, a simple reflection of the referent or its mimetic representation. Quite to the contrary, the referent is itself (77) produced by language as its own *effect* . . . language [like the lover] makes itself part of what it refers to (without, however, being all that it refers to). . . . The referent is no longer simply a preexisting *substance*, but an *act*, that is, a dynamic movement of modification of reality" (76–77). The sexual/textual experience results from the imbrication of terms, one term inextricably related to the others.

Yesterday when I was reading "Sous La Langue," I said, I should write a letter to Nicole. But my lover said, you just did. And I said yes, but I mean to write her a letter here.

Dear Nicole,

I should use this opportunity to ask you difficult questions. I want to know if you really did it or if you are just writing about it, whether writing (or reading) make you wet and excite to orgasm. Do you consider the spaces like the distance between two bodies, the gap between words or letters on a page or in the mind, or the slippage between words and their meanings? Do the words start with the letter "L"? Lesbian. Lover. Lust. Letter. Does "L" also mean something different to you? Langage. Langueur. Lire. Livre.

My trouble is this: it's easy to see how art is like life, but it is not as easy to see how life is like art, how life is made by/in language. Every lesbian I know thinks that she would rather do it than write or read about it. Wouldn't you? Is it because they are not writers? Or that they don't stop to think how, when they move from kissing to caressing to fucking (because they are not necessarily in this order) at least from the moment of engagement (or even engazement), they are inscribing the text of their desire in letters which, although they may fade, are carefully imprinted on their lover's body, designed to relate a narrative of power and longing which bears within it other such plots: lesbian intertextuality. If this is the case, then my question is superfluous (overflowing its bounds, excessive as well as unnecessary).

Love,

L

A problematic, though common, assumption informs my discussion of "Sous La Langue." It stems from a view of desire for/ as consummation figured in terms of arousal, satisfaction and release—a way of thinking that suggests that the object can be known and having it can put an end to desire, a way of writing that is traditionally representational. Brossard's *écriture de dérive*, described by Karen Gould as "a writing that is both *derived from* and *adrift*" (88), attempts to sidestep such notions in its pursuit of a new trajectory for lesbian : writing that marks the gap between the "signifier and signified, between language and lived experience in her texts" (88) through the white scene of passionate engagement.

Olga Broumas's "She Loves" offers another approach to figuratively, syntactically, and rhythmically representing the textuality of bringing her lover to orgasm. Following "I tap. I slap. I knee, thump, bellyroll," Broumas begins a course of action—an intricated accumulation of abundance, really—that sweeps over two stanza breaks as its sexual energy mounts:

> Her song is hoarse and is taking me,
> incoherent familiar path to that self we are all
> cortical cells of. Every o in her body
> beelines for her throat, locked on
>
> a rising ski-lift up the mountain, no
> grass, no mountaintop, no snow.
> White belly folding, muscular as milk.
> Pas de deux, pas de chat, spotlight

on the key of G, clef du roman, tour de force letting,
like the sunlight lets a sleeve worn against wind, go. (65–66)

The syllables in the line pile up like the sound in her lover's throat. They overrun the stanza breaks, mounting in the final two long lines. The figures are not determinative: what is the mountain without a crest and how does sunlight play on a worn sleeve? From o to go, the sounds are dispersed. The sonorous key of G collects the notes and recalls the G spot, the site of female ejaculation. I can't help but think that this must be *jouissance.*

Dear Olga,

Thank you for sending me *Perpetua.* I especially like the poem "She Loves." And the Os. The lover's hoarse cry, the o of letting . . . go—how the sound, instead of collecting itself in a culmination, culminates in a letting go.

Olga, what you started in *Beginning with O:* oceans, eros, oregano, omega, Io. As you say there, words

> . . . tear at you
> spirant by sonorant
> tongue by tongue
>
> some weird mutation of orgasm
> a spasm (30)

In your new book it seems that you have come around to begin again, but with a difference: the qualities of love and language, the sound of the sounds, are less troubled, the rage and pain of exposure, bitterness and betrayal diminished.

When you were in Tuscaloosa you said, "a poem begins for me as a somatic reality." It is as though your body has changed, registering other vibrations, like a voice pitched to a new tuning fork. Is the difference a difference within your body which now demands its expression in an/other language? Do the words of pleasure in the lexicon finally exceed those of sadness, no matter what language you choose? Do your lovers' faces now substitute themselves for those of the gods?

Love,
L

Representation amounts to a language effect from /in which the thing itself, indeed even as referent, escapes. Fugitive. As with lovers, in the relationship of language and act or event, there is always failure. Nothing is what/as it seems (semes). Could it be, I worry, that what I say is not what I mean at all?

One's relationship to (textual) subjects is con/textualized in such a way that certain subjects or perspectives are considered forbidden, desiring, seductive. Proscription as power effect. But in the expression of the forbidden, the affective force of the violated taboo, the repressed subject, surfaces.[2] Erotic energy is released in the letter, even when the writer and the reader are lesbians. A violation takes place; and a violence.

Unbelievable though it seems, eroticism and writing lend themselves to explication according to analogous rules. Love and words create pleasure similarly. As Felman explains it, "Meaning, in fact, can be accompanied by pleasure only on condition that it *fall* from one level to another. In other words, the passage from one textual plane to another is on the order of a skid or a fall" (117–18). The field or ratio for tortion establishes itself in this way; there is one level and another, one speed and a faster one. The body or the word as torque converter, site of differential tension—(sem)erotic skid.

I apply my energy to the love project. Torque: the twisting and turning in the driving tension of my passion for you. Lesbian : vision is a torque differential machine, relating me to you. Because I am always approaching you/we who have no definition, the absence of definition consigns us to more writing, no endings, more talking, mountains without tops, threatening the de/nominative project of "the known."

torque—a. The moment of a force, a measure of its tendency to produce torsion and rotation about an axis, equal to the vector product of the radius vector from the axis of rotation to the point of application of the force by the force applied. b. Broadly, a turning or twisting force. [From Latin *torquere*, to twist . . .]

Your lover, I am a *torque converter*—a "device for changing the ratio of torque to speed between the input and output shafts of a mechanism." I grab your legs with mine, holding them in place, while our bodies, intertwined, spin and whirl around that fixed point. For a moment, my body converts the speed of you and the speed of me to us in the torsion of lesbian : love, where we can move together in the same field, the bed, and the fuck, or, perhaps, pass together into some other field, some dangerous fantasy, to transgress a boundary. Playing on our perimeters, we explore fission and fusion, where one stops and the other begins. Georges Bataille says that "the ultimate meaning of eroticism is fusion, the suppression of the limit" (143). I say lesbian love, from the outset, defies the limit, and fission can also produce an undeniable rush.

torsion—n. 1.a. The act of twisting or turning. b The condition of being twisted or turned. 2. The stress caused when one end of an object is twisted in one direction and the other end is held motionless or twisted in the opposite direction. [Late Latin *torsio*, from *torsus*, "twisted." See *torsade*.]

torsion balance—An instrument with which small forces, as of electricity or magnetism, are measured by means of the torsion they produce in a wire or slender rod.

Dear L,

How should I address you in my love letters? L, my lesbian(ism), my Lover, my love, through the glistening pip, the shining tendril (of) your desire for me, the slender rod registering the relation of your frequency and mine. My task is to convert you and me to us. You are you. I want you to be separate so that I can feel the thrill of taking (you) over, composing you/ me/mine/ours. For a moment I construct you/me: inseparable, just as I write the word "us" or we—a rewriting of you/me. A momentary substitution. The "you" standing in for you is the machinery that makes these letters possible. Overdrive : overwrite. What is passion without the dream of a resistance, a difference even ever so slight, to be overcome as I push you down on the bed, a distance to be bridged as I cover your body with mine, I orchestrate and perform my desire on your smooth skin, I play the fuck master and take you (in). Perhaps there is not even a sound.

Love,
L

The text of this letter, or the letter of this text, anticipates pleasure, makes pleasure, at least for the lesbian lover/reader, as it predicts it. Roland Barthes, in *The Pleasure of the Text*, maintains that "the text of pleasure is not necessarily the text that recounts pleasures; the text of bliss is never the text that recounts the kind of bliss afforded literally by an ejaculation. The pleasure of representation is not attached to its object" (55). The pleasure in/of the letter has no attachment to its object because there is no essential connection between the sender and the receiver or the word and the thing it represents. Still, the search for each word elicits the memory of you in your absence, and I write (or read) not you, but *of* you, *with* you—the closest I can get. I spell out the conjugation of your memory in the present.

How is the pleasure of the "lesbian" text materialized? Is it that a "lesbian" reads something of herself in it? What is there, for example, in Becky Birtha's "Plumstone" that is erotic and lesbian?

> eating a plum
> I tongue the tight skin
> drawn seam
> that halves this globed

whole in two
it's midnight
blue outside
but when I bite in
bursting
with wet red flesh
the juice dripping down
my fingers sweet
sticky sticky
sweet pulp
engorged I
fill my mouth
eat it down
eat it down
all the way to the plumstone (11)

The poem achieves its eroticism by means of analogy. The speaker claims to be eating a wet, juicy, sticky plum, to be breaking in on its turgidity for her own pleasure and consumption. The sensations described—the feel of the tongue on the plum, the words chosen—"I tongue," "I bite," "eat it down/eat it down," offer us an alternative reading on the subject of oral sex. Eroticism requires the substitution for the literal, pleasurable but not erotic, act of eating the lush fruit. There is fruit and "fruit."

But what, besides the title of the collection—*By Word of Mouth: Lesbians Write the Erotic*—signals a *lesbian* (sem)erotic? Eating a plum can be "like" tonguing balls, the globed scrotum, but where, in the heterosexual paradigm, is the plumstone, and the "sticky sticky" fleshed fruit? The figure upon which the analogy turns suggests female genitalia, "the red wet flesh," and the lesbian content depends upon our taking the first-person speaker of the lyric poem as a gendered stand-in for the poet herself. Woman plus woman equals a different sexual mathematics.

While man/woman/homosexual are effects of a heterosexual sex/gender system, the lesbian is something else.[3] There is a subversive ring to the word "lesbian," particularly when she is a

lover, when she is sexually active and not invisible or (in)different.[4]
She writes erotic letters to her lover, she kisses and bites her on
the back of the neck: their transgressions multiply, ecstatically.
The eroticism of "Plumstone," then, emerges in part from the
lesbian reader's dual identification: she is lover and beloved. The
lesbian subject position affords multiple pleasures through the
ease with which one imagines being the one who is eating, or
the "plum" being eaten, or a third person viewing the women
lovers' scene.

(Sem)erotics is the energy of the excess produced by the
substitutive quality of words, where word stands (in) for "thing,"
and word substitutes for word, as in metaphor, or word elides
word, slides into word, as in metonymy. The elision of sex/
textuality fuels the project of desire. According to Guattari, "to
write one thing and before another, that means participating in
a chain, in a chain of love as well" (66). Love as a language chain.
What and how does the lover write on/in the beloved's body?
The left over, the left out, the extra, produces an energy effect,
a residual feeling that is mutual, a shadow form that we allow
ourselves to take as a suggestion that there really is a "real." The
body, sexual pleasure, orgasm, exceed the letters which are
chosen to stand in for them, as do all objects of representation.
Language exceeds and/or reduces the s(c)ene; words slip and
slide into and over one another. They suggest more or other
than the simple representation of the literal. Plumstone to clitoris, and vice versa. The ornamented body, love elaborated and
invented, the fiction (of) A.

(Sem)erotics—the sexual torsion of semantic order, of words
on the page. Tension/torsion/torque—the energy twists, the me-
chanics of the dialectic of physical love. Even in my dreams I
practice my task. We move against and with one another, bone
on bone, skin to skin, endlessly without words g(r)asping out
passion, constructing its ebb and flow. There was at the outset a
word beginning with a "D." I have no memory of it now. And
when we finished, I had forgotten even your name, and called

back through a litany of lovers until I came once again to you—
not out of a disrespect or newness, you are love now, but out of
the erasure deep affection makes, of what is not here and also of
what is, the absence that follows upon the exquisite intensity of
presence that passion composes and leads me to believe in.

The lover's task: Part of being me is loving you, constructing
your ecstasy, leading you to discover it in me, encouraging you
to want me to give you pleasure, just as I want you to take me
on, become the lover you imagine me to be. Love plots.

As Barthes would have it, absences, or suggestions of the
unseen, are even more erotic than presence or what is revealed.
He asks, "Is not the most erotic portion of a body *where the
garment gapes?* In perversion (which is the realm of textual
pleasure) there are no 'erogenous zones' (a foolish expression,
besides); it is intermittence, as psychoanalysis has so rightly
stated, which is erotic: the intermittence of skin flashing between two articles of clothing (trousers and sweater), between
two edges (the open-necked shirt, the glove and the sleeve); it is
this flash itself which seduces, or rather: the staging of an
appearance-as-disappearance" (*Pleasure* 9–10). For Barthes, the
space between, the suggestion of what is there but not yet there,
the visibly invisible, makes erotic claims.

Dear L,

I am wondering if Barthes is right, whether I find you sexier
when you are dressed or undressed, one of the differences between *off our backs* and *On Our Backs*. When I see you naked
on the bed, your legs opened up for me, your breasts, standing
in beautiful rounded form, nipples erect, I want to fuck you. I
know I can. But then, and perhaps this is like writing about the
erotic, when we are at a party and I look at you, how your shirt
falls away from your neck and down toward your breasts (I know
they are bare underneath, the surface glide of your skin is imprinted like a memory on my palm, I see the outline of your
nipples), you look at me and then turn your head away as you

smile, a look I know is only for me—I am yours. Why must I choose the more exciting practice? This and more: I want it all.

Love,

L

Your breasts, your naked body, interest me because they are the scene of prolongation, arousal. They invite me, like the text invites its reader, to linger rather than to conclude (the usual narrative interest), to sum up or to penetrate (the interpretive interest). Sex(t)ual cross purposes. In the section of *The Literary Speech Act* entitled "The Last Word of Scandal," Felman begins with a question and a provocative comment: "If the performative, in fact, is an event—a ritual—of desire, should we be surprised to learn that performative desire always takes as its model, rhetorically, the symbolics of sexual desire? . . . [T]he speech act is modeled on a metaphorics of the 'performance' of the sexual act" (Felman 108). If we follow a similar direction with respect to lesbian : desire, we might expect to employ an alternative metaphorics. Patricia Parker speaks of an "erotics of prolongation" (16).[5] What figures, vehicles, rhythms (ex)tend the passion of engagement? Perhaps the notion of caressing and exciting a text, rather than penetrating or being spent, might serve as the figure for the infinite coursing of desire that is lesbian reading and writing. I imagine an orgasm without end or an infinitely extended fore-pleasure where one becomes inseparable from the other. Worth noting is the dilatory aim of desire, how it defers the (con)summation and wants foreplay to go on forever:

dilation n. 1. The act or process of dilating; expansion; dilation. 2. The state or condition of being dilated or stretched. 3. *Medicine.* a. The condition of being abnormally enlarged or dilated. b. Dilation. 4. Expatiation in writing or speech.

The dilation of another "eye," one that usually eludes the masculine scopic economy, compels lesbian : desire.

In writing this, I pose a substitute for doing "it," make it last longer: it is repeatable (iterability is a key to signification), its meanings are inexhaustible (more so than in life?). Explaining the capacity of language to push back the frontiers of sense and non-sense, Ricoeur concludes that "there are probably no words so incompatible that some poet could not build a bridge between them; the power to create new contextual meanings seems to be truly limitless. Attributions that appear to be 'non-sensical' can make sense in some unexpected context. No speaker ever completely exhausts the connotative possibilities of his words" (95). The limitlessness of language and of sexual variation produces new meanings, other as yet imagined plotlines.

I approach the passage and provide a rhythm, reading faster, then slower and slower still. I defy the narrative conventions and skip around, reading the orgasm before the foreplay, returning to the parts I like best. Desire supplies a "style." The categorical "break" creates fuel, or in Guattari's words, "A break in sexuality —therefore homosexuality, a becoming woman, as addict, as missionary, who knows? It's a factory, the means of transmitting energy to a writing machine" (63). Like words on a page, two lesbians come together, *co*-incidences as events unexpected, in the wonderful variety of co-occurrence. Lesbian twins coming together and *coming* together.

(Sem)erotics: a coming together and a coming apart. Fusion and fission. As Brossard puts it in *Surfaces of Sense:*

once the line has deviated from its normal path (the course of reason), anything can happen; and it can take any sort of turn (lively or slow) with each new beginning.

it is for this reason that the wide circle of deviants is formed—tear to tear, mouth to mouth, ear to ear, word for word, day after day. (22)

Beyond the constraints of the "normal," the logical and reasoned snares of "sense," anything can happen. The traces loosen and I can read and write another story. Brossard sums up her project as follows: "spire to spire emotion: I conceived the inconceivable geometry: *the ardent form"* (*Surfaces* 23). Cunt to cunt: genre and gender demand something else, another passion. To me there is something arbitrary about the designation of a particular geometric form. Ardor, its roots almost as old, rather than the geometry of the shapes it finds, commands my attention. A passion that burns, creating its igneous transmutations. That's why this book is as it is.

Dear L,

If you enter the right (properly improper?) frame of mind, you can feel the excitement I experience as I consider lesbian : passion and write this list of lovers, joining them to others, actual and fictional. Every lesbian : writing the erotic inscribes her lovers' names, at some time or another:[6] sandy, alice, billie, julie, jean, carol, vonceil, sharon, maria, marly, karla, joanne, marcia, rose, daphne, betsy, gertrude, marie-therese, claude, barbara, sue, jan, virginia, naomi, valerie, nicole, marisa, vita, gayle, nancy, amy, jennifer, ellen, joan, minnie bruce, cynthia, adrienne, michelle, jeffner, namascar, elizabeth, olga, pat, annabel, rita, andrea, elliot, liana, lisa, audrey, kay, djuna, paula.

I could go on. I could disclose the secrets of so many others. What enigma creates the excitement of these (improper) names? Outlaws of pleasure, and more. Aren't you glad your name is here? And if it isn't, what will you do to add it?

Love,
L

SIX

X-Rated: Politics and Lesbian (Sem)Erotics

Like the star of a traditional porn film, the lesbian body is caught within a representational order which consumes her as fantasy at the same time it ensures her absence. Thus eclipsed, she becomes tangled between a twilight world where she experiences her self and a fluorescent world which degrades her into spectacle.

—Lynne Fernie, *Sight Specific* (25)

Literal means "that which is represented by letters." Taken literally. Taken to the letter. For we do take our bodies, our skin, our sweat, pleasure, sensuality, sexual bliss to the letter. From the letters forming these words emerge the beginnings of our texts.

—Nicole Brossard, *The Aerial Letter* (135–35)

Experiences aren't pornographic; only images and representations— structures of the imagination—are. That is why a pornographic book often can make the reader think of, mainly, other pornographic books, rather than sex unmediated—and this not necessarily to the detriment of his[her] erotic excitement.

—Susan Sontag, "The Pornographic Imagination" (49)

Whips.
Chains.
Spike heels.
Dildos.
Dungeons.
Leather.

What turns you on? This is only the beginning of my list. There should be pictures. We could discuss both the soft and the hard as ways to consider the question. Only the arbitrariness of the book separates these considerations from the previous chapter. To look again at eroticism, pornography and the question of sexual pleasure is to insist that the analysis of woman's pleasure is a subject yet to be adequately theorized by feminists, lesbian or not.

The figure of the "lesbian" produced in much lesbian-feminist discourse is a monochromatic type whose sexual (or asexual) virtue is overwhelming. She is never "caught looking" at or reading pornography, she disparages butch/femme roles and s/m practices, and she is wary of both penetration and sexual fantasies involving men. Conceived reactively, she is everything men are not—at least anatomically, socially, and spiritually, if not always athletically or materially. Sometimes she is also everything that heterosexual women are not, unless they are liberal, enlightened feminists who just happen to have found (or are still looking for) the one decent man to live with, marry, or date. Or who have only girl children.

Linda Williams, in *Hard Core*, points out one of the major flaws in the analyses offered by anti-pornography feminists. Basing their arguments on a "natural opposition," writers like Andrea Dworkin argue that women would be free of power's corruption if they somehow escaped the patriarchal context (the fundamental assumption of separatism). Williams continues:

The implications of Dworkin's argument—and of the anti-pornography feminist position in general—is that men are carnal, perverse, powerful, violent beings who "love murder" (Dworkin in Lederer 1980, 148), while women are asexual or gently sexual and even inherently lesbian beings. This argument suggests, erroneously I believe, that if female sexuality were ever to get free of its patriarchal contaminations it would express no violence, would have no relations of power, and would produce no transgressive sexual fantasies. (20)

One of the difficulties inherent in the anti-pornography position is that, when extended, it leads to the annihilation of lesbian sexual differences: it attempts to "lesbianize" all feminists and to homogenize all lesbian sexual practices, or at an even greater extreme—that represented by WAS, Women Against Sex—denies all sexual engagements.[1] These homogenizing moves produce considerable alienation in all directions.

In its effort to reclaim the clitoris and the lesbian from the realm of perversion, feminism has instituted another standard for normal sexuality. The norm for feminist sexuality is an egalitarian relation of tenderness and caring where each partner is considered as a "whole person" rather than as an object of sexual fantasy. This norm clearly devolves from feminist critiques of patriarchal, phallocentric sexuality. Since relations between the sexes are, in a feminist analysis, considered the equivalent of relations between class enemies, the egalitarian standard renders questionable whether any heterosexual relation (at least at this point in history) can be "normal."

Normal feminist sexuality is thus lesbian. (Gallop 107)

If every feminist were a lesbian, what would either of these words mean? What interests me here, however, is the specifically related problem of differences within the lesbian community as they are related to sexual pleasure. Something about sexual pleasure doesn't want boundaries or interruptions. A day in bed. Even the quick fuck issues from singlemindedness, a boundariless focus on the lover, a trajectory of desire pursued throughout the day—if only in the mind—anticipating the heat of skin on skin, the friction between two bodies in a tight embrace. The lover, then, is *like* an object of reflection, a point around which we organize our thoughts and affections as we compose our desire or as our desire composes us in the contemplation of the lover. When our meeting is a surprise, an extra pleasure, there is nothing that surrounds us in the moment of engagement. You and me, subject and object, subject wishing to be object of my lover's affection.

Dear L,

I am wondering how far I should go. That's always the question about sex, isn't it? From the beginning kids worry about "going all the way." What's "safe," like "safe sex"? Probably nothing. I can't think of any pleasures that are without dangers; surely there are some. But what is a thrill or a rush, anyway? Wanting it, wanting to "go all the way." And what is that for a lesbian—somewhere I/you/we have never been before? More? Faster? Harder?

PASSION + EXCESS (more/different) = EXCITEMENT.

How far do you want to go, baby? I am depending on you to know.

Love,

L

I suspect that little in my letter would offend the general lesbian reader. The conjunction of "danger" and "pleasure" could raise an objection. The comparatives—more, harder, faster—might be glossed as manifestations of a phallic economy (feminist sexologists caution against conceiving of sexual pleasure as "more" orgasms, and some separatists speak against any interest whatsoever in orgasm, regarding it as goal or achievement oriented, and therefore "masculine"). I contend that the "more," "harder" and "faster" of sex are not simply about phallic economies; they are about excess, something more terrifying because it is beyond the ordinary or the familiar, something beyond social conventions, beyond control, beyond "the language of control" which frequently marks feminist discourse (Diamond and Quinby 119). Perhaps it is actually the *beyond* of lesbian sadomasochism, or of any image or practice considered pornographic, that repels (terrifies) other feminists.

Mapplethorpe's most fearful-looking pictures are those with a sado-masochistic sexual plot. . . . Their revolt against the idea of the sexual secret is epic. And from the point of view of today, what also matters is how they tap and provoke that old tyrannical nonsense of a punitive system ruled by the gods—with supposed consequences which are said to be brought on when you decide for yourself what is right and wrong to do with your own body. (Sischy 84)

In her discussion of the pleasure/danger opposition, Mariana Valverde raises a key question: "To what extent do patriarchal relations determine our sexual fantasies and practices, and to what extent can we as individuals develop a 'free' sexuality?" (237). This question underlies the feminist debates about pornography, butch/femme roles and s/m. The positions taken reflect a complex grid of forces including age, feminist analysis, political ideology, relationships with heterosexual and homosexual men, past sexual experiences (including traumatic ones like incest and sexual abuse), and perhaps even individual libido. Feminist arguments against sadomasochism—and one might add separatist arguments against heterosexual intercourse in general —firmly place the woman in a masochistic relation to the male sadist, thus replicating structurally the power hierarchy (dominant male/submissive female) of the phallocentric world at large —the object of feminist critique—or what might be said to *constitute* "the feminist." (Similar dichotomizing conceptualizations also determine representations of butch/femme relationships, even in certain lesbian feminist discourses.) As Joan Hoff points out, radical feminists argue against what she calls "pornrotica" on the basis "that its very existence harms women by maintaining a patriarchal status quo and by projecting a subordinate and degrading view of women that often equates violence with virility for men and pain with pleasure for women" (31). The case of lesbian s/m threatens this argument at its foundation. Anti-pornography feminists, in order to maintain their position, must deny feminist agency to participants in and consumers of material depicting lesbian s/m, as well as their cohorts who endorse butch/femme roles. To enjoy doing or viewing lesbian s/m, the argument goes, is to display false consciousness, to have been brainwashed by patriarchal society, to succumb to what Hoff calls "sexist social-control tactics, disguised as sexual liberation, that are harming women" (35). Or as Sheila Jeffreys puts it in "Sexology and Antifeminism," experiencing sexual pleasure undermines a woman's ability to stage a "resistance to male power" (25).

Jill Dolan, however, suggests that views like Hoff's are reductive replications of the sexual opposition where the dominant male occupies one pole and the submissive female the other—a structure which, as the conventional wisdom has it, s/m and butch/femme roles depend upon and blatantly act out. Dolan contradicts this view: "All sexuality has a quotient of power. Sadomasochism takes power to extremes, or simply, by analogy, makes textual what is subtextual in many sexual relationships. Both as a paradigm of the culture's construction of gender, and as a sexual choice, s/m can be seen as a literalization of the power status inherent in the dichotomized male/female roles. First amendment issues aside, perhaps lesbian s/m offers an opportunity to explore the nature of power and sexuality apart from strict gender dichotomies" (171). Problems lurk in statements like this. I want to call them inescapable, but lesbians have been escaping them from the beginning (along with data on lesbian battering and lesbian child abusers).[2] Certainly, questions of power and sexual roles inhabit aspects of every relationship, and often remain the subtext of our most intimate moments: How often do you fuck? Who decides? How do you do it? Do you both find it satisfying? How is this negotiated, day to day, year to year? Do you talk about it? Why? Why not? When such questions concerning intimacy remain outside the ongoing process of our relationships, I guarantee that they are nonetheless answered by someone or something.

Dear L,

I'm still depending on you. I read an article in *Out/Look* called "Drawing the Line" by Kiss and Tell, a lesbian visual arts collective that explores pornography and censorship issues. I wanted to see their pictures and to read women's responses (the ones in the "men's book" didn't seem very interesting).

Kiss and Tell asks important sex questions. The artist's statement ended this way: "Is there a line that to cross means you're on the other side? Is everyone on this side on the same side of the line?" (8) Some women who saw the exhibit "drew the line" at bondage. What side of that line are you on? Am I there with you? Do you want me to be?

We crossed a line sometime last summer. I can tell from what they say that we left others behind, and I keep wondering lately who we joined. I think I'm afraid to find out. I do know that on the other side of the line is another line. We're a long way from it. We don't even seem to want to approach it very quickly. Does being here mean that you want to be here and that you know how far you are willing to go?

I'm waiting for your reply.

Love,

L

Arguing along lines similar to Dolan, Linda Williams and Parveen Adams maintain that more play within the role structure is evident than the simple sado-male maso-female reduction suggests.[3] Even when the woman occupies the masochistic position, or reads a text in which a woman holds that position, interpretations other than (though not as easy as) the traditional role-bound ones are quite possible. Williams notes, for example, "one answer to the question of how the female spectator identifies with the masochistic scenario is, first of all, that she does not necessarily identify only with and exclusively with the woman who is beaten; she may also, simultaneously, identify with the beater or with the less involved spectator who simply looks on. And even if she does identify only with the tortured woman, she might identify alternately or simultaneously with her pleasure and/or her pain" (215). There is an agency (activity) and pleasure to be gained from the part, and it is harder to determine than the "pleasure" a heterosexual woman gains from her socially validated and rewarded role as the presumedly "passive" sexual partner—a set of presumptions that also bear questioning. (It matters, in other words, where you stand in relation to the lines that you or others draw.)

Judith Butler underscores and extends the implications of this point through her differentiation between representation and fantasy: "The reason why representations do not jump off the page to club us over the head, although sometimes we fantasize precisely that, is that even pornographic representations as textualized fantasy do not supply a single point of identifcation for their viewers, whether presumed to be stabilized in subject-positions of male or female. Indeed, the postulation of a single identificatory access to the representation is precisely what stabilizes gender identity" ("Force" 114). The kind of "gender trouble" suggested in "cross-identification" behaviors (lesbian s/m, the dominatrix, butch/femme roles) is suppressed by the anti-pornography, anti-s/m factions within feminism in the interest of political consistency—a consistency which, according to Elizabeth Fox-Genovese, does not characterize feminist arguments in general. Unlike the traditional male (read "sadist") of everywoman's (read "masochist") daily or nightly drama, the sadist in a consentual s/m scene has the obligation to satisfy her partner (LeMasters 26). We could even claim that there is a certain subversiveness in the fact that each partner must play for the other's desire and pleasure.

> *Of course, I reared my head from the page. I must test. How was I reacting? What was this Oc [woman in pornographic text] to me: self-subject-identified or submissively, supinely subjected object?*
>
> *The answer was, for the first time since I had entered my maze of queries, totally clear. While I read, I was (except when my grumbling intellectual accompaniment held me off, which it did in rather the same bumpty, fending way as those ludicrous but slightly imagination catching quasi-deck-quoits must have held off Oc's thighs one from the other) Oc.*
>
> *Unhappily, a contradictory answer was no less clear. While I read, I also saw Oc—from the outside.* (Brophy 105)

I was and I saw Oc, Brigid Brophy's character confesses to herself. Where is the line between being and seeing, between the inside and the outside?[4] Between experience, fantasy, and representation? Are they separable? Who and what are aligned with sadomasochistic practice and not? What is it about sado-masochism that leads lesbian feminists like Sheila Jeffreys to equate it with fascism? And why is it not only the acting out, the sexual practice, but also the textual and visual practices that offends? Pornography, after all, as Angela Carter observes "is basically propaganda for fucking" (15), and lesbianism has always been, at least in some quarters, a sexual practice. In any case, according to many feminists and lesbian feminists, sadomaso-chism, as a particular manifestation of sexual interaction, is best kept in the closet and expunged from the repertoire of women's festivals, fantasy, the unconscious and representation. I can re-call no other lesbian sexual practice that boasts a book as well as numerous articles and a constant barrage of letters written *against* it. The specific geography of this resistance merits examination, if for no other reason than the fragmentation it marks in the feminist community (pro and anti-s/m and pornography forces each blaming the other), and perhaps as a way of understanding how this resistance to pornography relates to conservative efforts to limit public funding to certain artists, prominent among them the lesbian poets Audre Lorde, Minnie Bruce Pratt and Chrystos.

MORE. FASTER. HARDER.

Feminists have historically distinguished between eroticism and pornography, claiming the former for themselves and rele-gating the latter to a territory characterized as phallic or mascu-line. The most amusing commentary I've read on the differences between lesbian eroticism and pornography is Jan Zita Grover's "Words to lust by." She sees erotica as "good-girl writing," lesbian-feminism's answer to pornography. It offers a world of earnest lovers, aroused by "smouldering looks, clit-rubbing and -licking, and gentle explorations of the entire body" (21): "They enact their passion in rustic cabins, in nature, in beds. They want to see (themselves in) Her again, so relationship (ongoing, friendly, soulful) is important. The only toys entering into most lesbian erotica are feathers, steaming mugs of coffee (afterwards), candles (lit, stationary, in holders on table) and music. Sex is often described by allusion to flowers, fruit, waterfalls, pounding waves, illimitable oceans" (21). This catalogue, which one might take as a catalogue of what not to include in a lesbian novel, contrasts markedly with the pornographic "bad-girl writing" of "social constructionists." Here sex is dangerous and actively negotiated as the relations of pain and pleasure are explored in a world of masks, roles, and toys in variety and abundance: "The porn body is a terrain that can be traveled in many ways; surface and fissures that erotica usually ignores are its chosen *terra incognita*. Its central metaphor is the game: protagonists play out their sexual quest in costume, in assumed character, in the midst of crowded restaurants, gang bangs, motorcycle rallies, or amid the chosen isolation of dungeons, entombment and warehouses after midnight. The protagonist seeks not her like, but her other" (21). Formally, lesbian pornography, according to Grover, is self-reflexive, self-mocking, and self-conscious with respect to the conventions it employs. It turns on (itself), and invites the reader to do the same.

Grover's wit masks just how high the stakes are in this debate. Susanne Kappeler, for example, frames and punctuates her book-length analysis, *The Pornography of Representation*, with the inflammatory description of a black man's murder and the photographing of it by whites in Namibia. Kappeler uses this admittedly heinous event rhetorically to stand in for pornographic representations of women and to motivate the feminist case against such representations.[5] Similar in intent is Catharine MacKinnon's attack on representatives from FACT (Feminist Anti-Censorship Task Force): "The Black movement has Uncle Toms and Oreo cookies. The labor movement has scabs. The woman's movement has FACT" (12). From some perspective or other, anyone who crosses a line joins the class of traitors.

Audre Lorde in 1978 called eroticism the "opposite" of pornography, seeing them as "two diametrically opposed uses of the sexual" (*Sister* 55). She claims that pornography "is a direct denial of the power of the erotic, for it represents the suppression of true feeling. Pornography," she continues, "emphasizes sensation without feeling" (54). Much remains unspoken in Lorde's essay. Other than this characterization by negation, Lorde leaves pornography undefined. Is it that pornography "goes without saying" because we are certain to know what it is? Because it is too dangerous (messy/confusing) for us to define it? In some camps, "eroticism"—Carter calls it "the pornography of the elite" (17)—affords a feminist avenue for the exploration of sexuality in ways that are pure and exciting. Other writers such as Susie Bright conflate pornography and erotica; refusing an ethical hierarchy to distinguish between types of lesbian sexual practice or representation, Bright has no difficulty equating the terms. Discussing lesbian separatists at a 1979 Women Against Pornography conference, Ellen Willis offers a cunning argument that deserves broader consideration: "It seemed to me that their revulsion against heterosexuality was serving as the thinnest of covers for disgust with sex itself. In any case, sanitized feminine sexuality, whether straight or gay, is as limited as the predatory masculine kind and as central to women's oppression; a major function of misogynist pornography is to scare us into embracing it. As a further incentive, good cops stand ready to assure us that we are indeed morally superior to men, that in our sweetness and nonviolence (read passivity and powerlessness) is our strength" (465). Thus woman's victim status is reinscribed. Willis concludes that "in a male supremacist society the only obscenity law that will not be used against women is no law at all" (466). Jesse Helms's indictment of the lesbian poets, and the case of Audre Lorde in particular, seems to bear out Willis's view from more than a decade earlier.[6] Susan Cole extends the threat within more recent feminist debates in her desire to police the border between Canada and the United States, despite the censorship of lesbian and gay materials: "Gay and lesbian identity gets set back by keeping gay-positive sexual materials out of the country but fewer women are harmed when we keep the pornography out" (195). An unacceptably high price for an uncertain effect, I'd say.

But back to "eroticism" and "pornography." My dictionary differentiates between eroticism and pornography as follows: pornography excites "lascivious feelings," while eroticism arouses "sexual desire." When I get to the third meaning, however, the words begin to blur. *Eroticism*—"3.a. Abnormally persistent sexual excitement. b. Preoccupation with sex, especially in literature and art." I am off to see "lascivious," one of those words I have never written or said aloud. More L words: "lust; lewd; lecherous." There is something nonprocreative about "lasciviousness," as old a word as it seems. "Lust" was once nicer than it is now. *Lust*—"1. Sexual craving, especially excessive or unrestrained. 2. Any overwhelming desire or craving . . . 3. *Obsolete.* Pleasure, delight, relish." Intransitively lust is excessive. Yes, here we are again. The beyond, the too much. HARDER. FASTER. MORE. LONGER. *Lust*—"To have an inordinate or obsessive desire, especially sexual desire." I want too much. I want "it" too much. I want too much of it. And there is not even a word for me. (A *slut* is "a dirty woman," a "prostitute," like a *whore*—I give it away or sell it; then there is the clinical *nymphomania*—the "abnormal and uncontrollable desire by a woman" for sex.) I like my word for it, *nymphamania,* my lesbian obsession for those little *nympha* (yours are beautiful), the *labia minora,* and my obsession doesn't admit normalcy.

But *lechers,* those "given to excessive or promiscuous sexual indulgence," are men. Promiscuity suggests the randomness of their activities (outside the family?) as they indulge themselves. They have all the fun. *Indulge*—"1. To yield to the desires and whims of (oneself or another), especially to an excessive degree; humor; pamper. 2. To gratify or yield to; *indulge a craving for chocolate* . . . To allow oneself some special pleasure; indulge oneself . . . *indulge in an afternoon nap.*" There is a certain pleasure inscribed in these words of excess and indulgence. The examples depict a world of naps, pampering and chocolate. Indulgence: "*Sports cars are an expensive indulgence.*" The dictionary tells more than it knows.

Dear Baby,

It's Sunday afternoon and I want to eat chocolate, make love with you, and then take a nap. Afterwards, we'll get in the convertible and go for another ride. We'll listen to music: "nothing compares 2 U" (Sinead O'Connor's bad; she won't let them play the national anthem before her concerts), and "Me So Horny" from those dirty boys 2 Live Crew, "As Nasty as They Wanna Be" (that's a good motto, so it comes with a warning: explicit language contained. Some women only hear Bitch. Fuck. Bitch. Cunt. Cunt. when they listen), and maybe Shakespear's Sister singing "Heroine" and "Heaven Is in Your Arms" (Is heroin[e] a pun?: Is heaven?) Then there's Billy Idol. Can we play "White Wedding" with black people in the room?

Pornography and S/M are supposed to be decadent. Are there any similarities to us? Does this private party sound decadent enough, if we add other things to the chocolate and the sex? Indulgent is the word. What will the lesbian feminists say? No Margie Adams. No Alix Dobkin. We might not have any friends left after this. Will it matter to you?

Love,
Baby

In lesbian-feminist discussions of sexuality, PENETRATION is the issue, the "sticking point." The fear of taking things in (Bright 68) conditions the reaction of some lesbians to dildos, vibrators, certain vegetables, fisting, and as this list suggests, to s/m, the practice of which is at least implicitly associated with certain of these penetrating devices. *Penetrate*—"1. To enter or force a way into; pierce. 2.a. To enter into and permeate. b. To cause to be permeated or diffused; steep. 3. To grasp the inner significance of; understand. 4. To see through. 5. To affect deeply, as by piercing the consciousness or emotions." To pierce one's ears is common enough, even among lesbian feminists. But to be pierced or penetrated by another body, by a penis or an object controlled by another body is to open oneself up in a terrifying way, to risk disturbance or pain. Or perhaps to risk being affected deeply, "as by piercing the consciousness or emotions." Penetration involves a challenge to one's identity, to the integrity of the (closed off? intact? controlling?) body. A border crossing. A blurring of categories.

Sexuality activates a host of intra-psychic anxieties: fear of merging with another, the blurring of body boundaries and the sense of self that occurs in the tangle of parts and sensations, with attendant fears of dissolution and self-annihilation. In sex, people experience earlier substrates, irrational connections, infantile memories, and a range of rich sensations. We fear dependency and possible loss of control, as well as our own greedy aggression, our wishes to incorporate body parts, even entire persons. Having been told that pleasure threatens civilization, we wonder what if there is no end to desire? (Vance 5)

Doing sex risks the "no end," the going over the edge, and the "riskier" the sex, the deeper or more threatening (thrilling?) the abyss. Penetration, a stock feature of s/m, jeopardizes the "intactness" of the body, however illusory that belief in wholeness might be, but, paradoxically, when something goes into the body, an ecstasy is possible in which something also goes "out of the body," or the "body" as sentient subject, leaves itself, goes out of itself. Of course, we *know* that nothing or no one actually leaves the body (except as a result of natural processes). The pleasures of sex are its unreason, its contrariness, which frustrates our capacities to reason about our responses to pleasure and sexual practice, as subjects. I can taste the lusting animality of sweat, sex in Alabama summers, and feel again the torsion, writhing and sensation. Happiness settles in/on the body.

Was it bad, did it make her a bad person, to enjoy screwing clamps onto Doc's nipples or whipping her? Was she going to lose her mind and start killing people someday? Fluff knew that she didn't enjoy random infliction of pain. When the whip went astray, she wasn't excited, she got fussed. But did that have to do with the fact that Doc didn't like it, or was it because she didn't want to be clumsy or incompetent?

And where was all this leading them? How far could you go? Would there come a day when she would have to choose between being boring and being deadly?

Maybe Doc could have soothed some of her anxiety. But Fluff's pride prevented her from insisting that they talk this out. Besides, there were those glorious moments when she had no doubts. Times when they were covered with a single sheet of sweat, united in a struggle to wrest one more ounce of sensation out of Doc's flesh, compel the tongue to flick, slide, and probe one more orgasm, make her arm pump out one more fuck, whirl the cat for another ten minutes, when she could not tell who was making which noise because they were one creature. That was, Fluff told herself, all the answer and reason that she needed.

—Pat Califia, *Doc and Fluff* (239)

It is curious to me that no one wants to see s/m as a kind of sexual athletics—how much can I take? How far can I run? How much pain can I endure for the sake of pleasure? How high can I get? How many orgasms can I have or can my lover give me? One sets a limit and then exceeds it. (There it is again: EXCESS. Always a thrill.) As is the case with other instances of difference, we don't want to see the ways in which what we do (running farther and faster every day, for example, for pleasure) resembles what a lesbian s/m practitioner might do (increasing every day the amount of pain she can endure to gain increased pleasure). Or, as Pat Califia puts it in her introduction to *Macho Sluts:* "The prospect of a human body being rendered helpless, put under slowly increasing stress, so that the maximum amount of sensation can be run through skin, nerves and muscles, will always seem horrifying to some readers, not a fascinating attempt to bring out the body's stamina and grace" (25). Do we have to draw a line and cross it to get a thrill?

In the hope, one surmises, of curtailing lesbian sadomasochists' claims to feminism, the editors of *Against Sadomasochism* enlisted a number of U.S. feminism's most notable spokespersons. Some writers state that they do not regard s/m as "politically incorrect"; rather, their concern is to show how strictly incompatible it is with feminism—a distinction not elaborated. So few of the essays display well-reasoned challenges that I wonder how seriously the question has been engaged, whether or not it is possible to "reason" about this subject; the responses bear the marks of the position thought to be self-evident, that which goes without saying. As Gayle Rubin sums up the general range of objections to lesbian s/m in *Coming to Power:* "Sexual diversity exists, not everyone likes to do the same things, and people who have different sexual preferences are not sick, stupid, warped, brainwashed, under duress, dupes of the patriarchy, products of bourgeois decadence, or refugees from bad child-rearing practices" (223). And *Against Sadomasochism* contains its share of such allegations: s/m is an effect of the asymmetrical power distribution of patriarchal sexual ideology (4); it's "sick," clinically speaking (6), an addiction (9), violence (19); consent and its claims to role-playing are problematic (9); s/m rhetoric is used to support, mask and legitimize lesbian battering (21–22). Its reliance on dominance and submission (power imbalances) negates feminist aspirations to transform society, individuals and relationships (48).

Bat-Ami Bar On's "Feminism and Sadomasochism: Self-Critical Notes" is the most succinctly argued essay in the collection. She sees feminists as engaged in a debate concerning sexual liberation and the elimination of sexual violence and domination. Proponents in these two struggles are pitted against each other. Bar On claims that s/m is "morally objectionable" (72); she begins with the assumption that all parties (pro- and anti-s/m forces) are feminists. Her argument turns on the notion that there is a place for "progressive tolerance" of s/m, the position espoused by sexual libertarians. Using a series of premises, Bar On constructs a situation that requires s/m practitioners to demonstrate that "a sexual practice involving the eroticization of violence and domination and of pain or powerlessness does not thereby involve a violation of the right to determine what can be done with and to one's body" (77). The counter argument is, of course, that s/m practices are governed by consent and, unlike heterosexual sex in a patriarchal frame, controlled by the masochist (78); this is a position, Bar On notes, that feminism is not prepared to challenge, although she attempts to do so. She contends that s/m is governed by patriarchal *rules*, even though, despite feminists claims, it does not replicate, patriarchal *roles*. The roles are different because masochists frequently exercise control, not out of respect for feminist values, but from the participants' mutual interest "in encounters in which violence is eroticized" (80). Her final charge is that s/m fosters and relies upon fragmentation, which "stands in polar opposition to feminist visions. Feminism is about reintegration into an holistic mode of being and doing. We must affirm our commitment to the integrity of our bodies and our selves, a commitment which the vindication of sadomasochistic sexuality renders hopelessly compromised" (80).

Despite Bar On's claims, s/m does not replicate patriarchal rules. There is no "safe" word in life. Women are subjected to rule(s), whether they want to be or not. Sadomasochists too are subject to these rules as they move about in society at large. Bar On displays the limits of her argument when she notes: "A sadist with a reputation for noncompliance with the masochist control rule would probably be hard pressed to find a masochist in the sadomasochist community who would voluntarily enter into a sadomasochistic encounter" (79). It is precisely this dimension of volunteerism that is often absent from patriarchal rule(s).

Further, Bar On's insistence on the holistic approach, the "integrity" of bodies and selves, reiterates the feminist position of inviolability, limited exchange, impenetrability. Karen Rian offers a similar conclusion in her essay: "If cooperation, conscious self-determination and the elimination of power imbalances are feminist goals, then sadomasochistic relationships as *goals* are incompatible with feminist goals" (49). If . . . then. What about the "if"—cooperation, conscious self-determination and the elimination of power imbalances? These represent enormous assumptions on Rian's part, assumptions never argued with respect either to their desirability or their possibility.

The threat and the thrill of sex cannot be separated from
"power." Power is the ability of someone to do something, or to
refuse to do something, to or for you. You can give someone
power (your lover or friend); s/he can have it by virtue of a
subject position (employer, judge, member of socio-politically
dominant race or class, parent, teacher), or s/he can assume it,
take it because s/he wants it (upwardly mobile individual, lover,
criminal). Along these lines, consent means the power to refuse.
The dilemma is that we do not fully know our own feelings. The
power of the unconscious is such that we can give consent when
we do not really want to, or don't know that we want to, or even
believe that we did when we didn't. To admit the incongruence
of act and desire is to unsettle the questions of pornography and
sexual practice and to open the possibility for other writings of
the (lesbian) body. Amber Hollibaugh, Gayle Rubin and Joan
Nestle, among others, have been pointing this out all along.

I would be less than honest if I did not acknowledge what I
see as the knotty problems elicited by some s/m practitioners:
the use of Nazi paraphernalia, recalling the Holocaust; slave/
master terminology which offend blacks and whites who are
sensitive to the racial crimes of slavery. These features of s/m are
easier to explain than it is to ask some members of the lesbian/
feminist communities to accept them, if by that we mean to
regard them without anger, fear or horror. These responses are
no more easily revised than the responses of sadomasochists to
certain scenes and fantasies. This suggests a more general problem in much lesbian feminist discourse on sexuality: the denial
of or disregard for the unconscious, a function of feminism's
rejection of Freud. It makes us poor interpreters, fostering the
confusion of life and art, mistaking the pornographic text, a
discursive representation or image, a visual representation, for
the act itself (also there to be "read") upon one's lover or neigh-
bor,[7] and the planned, scripted scene from the often random
acts of everyday life. Pornography, as Andrew Ross observes in
No Respect, mediates between "real sexual activity" and psychic,
fantasmatic events. It produces its effect by means of "the *re-*

formed props of psychical reality; vestigial, and thus only partially acceptable, memory traces of prelinguistic events, primal fantasies, scenes of violent origin and castration, fragmentation and destruction of corporeal unity, etc." (200). From this psychic storehouse, pornographic texts and sadomasochistic scenes derive their erotic charge, their varying capacities to affect individuals. It is important to keep in mind that the psychic material Ross describes comes to us only in disguise, and thus is difficult to revise, as feminists such as Sheila Jeffreys repeatedly urge, in the interest of bringing it into line with any specific polemic.

Politically correct sexuality is a paradoxical concept. One of the most deeply held opinions in feminism is that women should be autonomous and self-directed in defining their sexual desire, yet when a woman says, "This is my desire," feminists rush in to say, "No, no, it is the prick in your head; women should not desire that act." But we do not yet know enough at all about what women—any women—desire. The real problem here is that we stopped asking questions so early in the lesbian and feminist movement, that we rushed to erect what appeared to be answers into the formidable and rigid edifice that it is now. (Nestle, "Fem" 234)

As Nestle so brilliantly reminds us, much in the relationship between feminism and sexuality is uncertain. Thus the notion of a feminist "position" on pornography, butch/femme roles, or s/m seems premature or at best provisional, to be called into question as soon as it is articulated. What seems certain to me, however, is that feminism cannot afford, in its ignorance of the many unsettled and unsettling sexual questions, to function as the thought police or "dictator[s] of desire" (Nestle, *Restricted* 117), either in the form of supporting anti-pornography legislation that people like Jesse Helms can then use against us, or to channel (women's) desire into appropriate avenues and destinies, replicating in some reactive or oppositional form the suppression of women's expressions of desire that has occurred for centuries. Someone pointed out, and it is true, that both

Dworkin and I conflate pornography and erotica. But she conjoins them in order to rule all of it out, while I want to collect all
of it together (to LOOK)—to understand what I mean, as a
lesbian feminist, when I write "I desire." For now, I want all of
it, and more. If it is premature to close the question of lesbian
feminism's position(s) on specific sexual practices and represena-
tions of them, the best I can offer is a number of alternative
endings, which only suggest new beginnings for future debate:

1. Carol LeMasters scatters challenging questions throughout
her essay. They are gifts—free, unanswered, often unexplored.
About s/m: "Can there be humiliation if all is a gift? Can there
be violation if there is no concept of closure? Can one be used if
all is freely chosen?" (22). About power and egalitarian relationships: "What is 'real' power? Are we to want it or not? Or only
certain kinds? In certain areas?" (23). About butch/femme roles:
"Even as far as gender roles are concerned, is the butch only a
replica of men? Is she not already something other, a unique
self-creation? Likewise, even as a lesbian claims a male privilege
in making love to a woman and yet remains entirely a woman,
may not someone claim an aggressive sexual role and remain
woman-identified?" (28). (This catalogue of questions offers an
agenda for work. Imagine what is required to address one of
these queries; nonetheless, some of us take up with confidence
our positions in the sex debates.)

2. Perhaps, contrary to Sheila Jeffreys's views, the goal of a
feminist revision of sexual pleasure lies along other more "perverse" lines—pleasure without a proper end or function. As
Linda Williams explains it, when sexual pleasure "dispenses with
strictly biological and social functions and becomes an end in
itself; when it ceases to rely on release, discharge, or spending
for fulfillment; when a desiring subject can take up one object
and then another without investing absolute value in that object;
and finally, when this subject sees its object more as exchange
value in an endless play of substitution than as use value for
possession—then we are in the realm of what must now be
described as a more feminine economy of consumption" (Wil-

liams 273). (Why did she have to say that about the "more
feminine economy"?)

3. Then there's Jan Grover's projection at the end of her
essay. She claims that the issues of our sexual future and its
representations will be argued on altogether different ground by
young, mainly urban, activists in Queer Nation whose slogan is
"We're here, we're queer, get used to it": "These young post-
lesbian, post-dyke, post-gay, post-homosexual, avowedly post-
postmodernists—white, black, Asian, chicano y chicana, latino
y latina—have beheld their elders' censorship and porn wars,
battles between men and women, and are dumbfounded: they
are *queers,* and their self-identification as queers embraces and
transcends every contradiction described above. They are large.
They contain multitudes. They're our future. And they've barely
begun writing" (23). (I like this writing that is yet to come, more/
other writing; I like the future possibility suggested in what we
do not have yet, what will take us by surprise.)

4. In the pornography issue of *Semiotics,* Berkeley Kaite takes
Robert Stoller's *Observing the Erotic Imagination* as her point
of departure. She begins her essay with the following sentence:
"The pornographic photograph is a 'published dream' " (79). As
a "dream work," then, from the realm of "private consumption,"
the pornographic photo "comes replete with its own symbolic,
subversive, ambiguous and repressed association" (79). This notion of the dream and Ross's comments on the unconscious
suggest to me one of the problems in feminist and lesbian feminist considerations of sexual pleasure. We share with gay theory
the silencing of the psychological, as Greenberg notes: "Even if
one rejects specific psychological explanations for homosexual
orientation one may still find in the notions of ambivalence, the
unconscious, conflict between impulse and prohibition, gender
identification, and psychological defense mechanisms conceptual
tools whose implications for hostility to homosexuality may be
worth exploring" (495). In the interest of theorizing the feminine, as distinct from the masculine, as a means of restoring or
establishing female agency, out of the desire to repudiate psy-

choanalytic treatment of women, and lesbian women in particular, feminist theorists have preferred to deny the unconscious and dreams, in favor of such notions as "self-actualization," "empowerment," and identity. The unconscious might be the great unspoken subject, the unmentionable (non)subject of most feminist and specifically lesbian theory in the United States today. To admit the unconscious means that we cannot so confidently and successfully plot our present and future. It threatens from the start the project of radical redesign and change, the singular secure identity, and the territory of the "known."[8]

5. Then again, it might be that the proliferation of sexual roles and interests, demonstrated in the persons inhabiting LeMasters's questions, the answerers, the queers of Grover's projection, the feminist pleasure seekers of Williams's text, and others not included or even yet imagined, will explode through their freewheeling diversity, the very categories of sexual roles and attendant pleasures, the permissible and the impermissible. Maybe we will enter an age of the Derridean "one sex for each time." The result could cause *real* "gender trouble" (Butler), where it becomes impossible to ascribe one form of behavior and/or pleasure to individual "types" or socio-political groups, or to know what one enjoys by virtue of membership[9]—the effect of which might be an explosion of pornographic writing in the service of a nonexploitative (Soble) and diversely pleasurable (lesbian) sexuality.

Dear L,

I've been reading the personals in *On Our Backs*. They make me want to go downstairs and drag you up to the bedroom.

For the first time, I thought about answering one of them. These lesbians WANT. They want all kinds of things. They're asking for a femme, a heavyset butch of color, a cool neo-butch (à la k.d.), an ultra-butch top, a busty femme, a hot 'n' hungry bottom, scenes, spankings, lesbian cocks, hair, hot sex, satisfaction (which we all know is hard to get). There are things they don't want: S/M dykes, femmy butches (they want them "pure" butch). Somebody else wants to write to erotically awakened dykes who don't smoke, aren't alcoholic or unhealthy. Does smoke travel from my house to yours, through the mail? Do you think this ad is really about writing?

These letter writers come from all over. Mostly they want lesbians who are 20 to 40, only a few say they don't care. I guess I don't fit in that category, but then what would I go as, anyway? Do you know? You'll have to tell me in case the right ad appears.

Love,

L

SEVEN

Body Talk: Lesbian Speculations on "Extra"Textual Letters

No one has imagined us.
> —Adrienne Rich, "Twenty-One Love Poems," in
> *The Dream of a Common Language*

Some say alright all but one way of loving, another says alright all but another way of loving . . . I like loving, I like all the ways any one can have of having loving feeling in them. Slowly it has come to be in me that any way of being a loving one is interesting and not unpleasant to me.
> —Gertrude Stein, *The Making of Americans*

We cannot hide from ourselves the fictional character of the first A.
> —Nicole Brossard, *These Our Mothers*

Dear L,

My title *(Sem)Erotics* opens a space for writing (about) lesbian : letters and lesbian : love. In all honesty, I am writing the book to get to this chapter, or perhaps even beyond it. But this is the chapter that is misunderstood, its relation to the literary, the political, mis-taken, while summation and extension, effects of its placement, are insisted upon.

I refuse to recognize both the lastness and the irrelevance of these "extra" letters. I write my chapter in relation to (because of, in the shadow of the letters—words and texts—that have come before). I am writing with. Surrounded.

I know that there is more to come. There is more (to say about) lesbian : writing, just as we have not yet enumerated the

variations on lesbian : eroticism. The uninvented, the unima-
gined remain. The historically uninvited must be invited to
speak.

FORE)

(This is about speculation, how I imagine what will interest
my lover, turn her on; and then . . . seduction, a seduction in/to
the letter.)

The effort of the *fore-* wants to precede the letter, to imagine
a feeling be-fore sex, to anticipate what I will say and the positions we will take, what I will do to her, what I want her to do to
me. An elaborate(d) invention, a complex fiction. Fore!—-told.
Look out ahead.

The *fore-* is the scene of intention, where I reach toward what
I don't really have yet, be-fore I imagine or accept the fiction of
"A"—the initial form that makes discourse possible, that founds
the conceit, so I can write letters to you, my lover. I invent the
scene of possibilities, a speculative fiction.

What if the language handed down for generations does not
contain you, or what it does say about you, what it sums up in
that one word, is rarely spoken or written, and when it is, the
inflection is all wrong, suggesting little more than spitefulness
and cruelty? Language deceives and language discloses; words
speak and words silence. They pose the challenge of what might
follow the letter L, how to invent a lesbian and what she means
to her lover. How to know one when you see one; how to read
and write her story.

The creation of categories requires the production of discourses about them. Hence, the importance of "LESBIAN,"
"LESBIAN : WRITING," "LESBIAN : READER," "LESBIAN
: LOVER." The elaboration of meaning: does it precede or follow
the letter? Because "we" are always approaching "us," I speculate in an absence of definition. I make words, writing and more
writing, to fill the lack and the imprecision (the unlikeliness of
sense) with specification, to create variations on the possible

through the shuttle of incalculable losses and gains as we translate each other, me to you, you to me. No one ever told me what my lesbian destiny could be, so I invent us. The terror I find in this results from language's utter dependence on and independence from the world. Flying (almost) blind.

How, beginning in absence, erasure or negation, do we raise this alienated writing to an art? Iterability counts: once, twice, three times. Saying it, over and over, in our own ways helps make it so: L, L, L, L. Dear L, we need to play it again and again and again, patiently recording the variations in our tunes. I want to count my ancestors, to include their texts in mine. I start here by reading one word after another, writing one letter after the next, constructing a long and varied correspondence, (ex)posing myself and you. I am going to speak in tongues, with my tongue, trying to make room for other tongues, different registers, which, when voiced serially, through harmonics and dissonance, make all sense and non(e). One thing I can say about this book: it will always be (my) LESBIAN : WRITING.

SEX)

Dear L,

When I fucked you at the Big Sur Inn I turned electric—green like the ocean glass ring you wear, the neon blues and pinks of unnatural materials, the metallic tints of space age metals that have never seen the ground. Nothing hand-made has ever been this beautiful. It must have been the ever-polite silence of close quarters that transliterated the sounds of pleasure into other forms—geometric, extraterrestrial, spatial landscapes of lesbian : love. This despite (or because of) Big Sur's elemental excesses—rocky shore, sea, limitless sky—observed year after year, but never appearing "natural."

So we went on (coming) on and on and on.

Surely we will keep returning.

Love,

L

This scene invites speculation. A lot can be said and done about it. Painters, they say, go to France for the light, its peculiar brilliance or clarity on the Mediterranean. But what is light to the writer, who, as often as not, composes a letter to her lover after dark, sometime past the day's end, in review, as a labor of memory or longing to have her again. (My lover calls it a "labor for love.") The rhythms of repetition, sex games, excitement: how pleasure makes more pleasure. Happiness writes itself in that.

(GAMES

she loves me she loves me not she loves me she loves me not she loves me she loves me not she loves me she loves me not she loves loves loves loves loves me
　　petal after petal after petal
　　Dropping each petal in the love game, she invents her lesbian : lover. They sit next to each other, counting on the minutes ahead. They tell each other the stories of their lives. They smile and touch, they kiss and tell some more. They shine.
　　Nicole Brossard says, "A lesbian who does not reinvent the word is a lesbian in the process of disappearing" (*Aerial* 122). Imagine (that is, in one sense, to conjecture, a variant of speculation) or Invent (to come upon). And let's get it right: We are here to stay.

GOTTA GET . . . PHYSI)

I am your lesbian : lover—and who/what is the lesbian behind "lesbian"? The one inscribed in lesbian : writing? There are no hermeneutic victories here, no texts put to rest, their authors discovered and interpreted once and for all. As a lesbian : reader, I am, as you are, the scene of lesbian : writing. I make sense of it, knowing there is more to come. I am one of those I write about, the subject of my own sentence. I live on the page, becoming what my writing tries to materialize, to literalize, to make present at least in the moments of writing and reading. They make me so.

Some days I have little interest in the abstract "Lesbian." I want mine with skin—chocolate or creamy, soft, her eyes brown or green flecked, arms strong. My girl has cunt, clit, lips, tongue —wet and warm. She shares.

I make her skin shine.

(-CAL

Like an astronomer studying the spectra of other galaxies, I try to read your colors, the red of divergence, the blue of convergence, going and coming. I want to know where and how we stand, or lie. I work close up. No telescope.

I see the book of my lesbian : lover's body. As already scripted, that is, understood and felt in someone's words, it writes to me —doing love—one letter to another. It is written in a language I think I can read, and write. We study each other together, perfecting our letters. When I connect them into a lover's alphabet, what meanings can I read there? And my lover—how does she read my hand : writing?

Doing love is a form of speculation—on the body, on the moment, on what is to come. It is an inscription on the lover's body in the name of desire, like characters written on a page, or a love letter I will send or not send.

EX-)

Ex = X (lover): Ex(it) lover

Ex-change

Ex/pressions—pressure to articulate, insisting in the brain, bone or tongue. The ribs of the chest: compression. Ex/tension: circulating the clit.

Ex-emplar: (L)
Ex-cavation
Ex-hilaration
Ex-cre(a)tion
Ex-pansion
Ex-orbitant Ex-stasies of L

The lesbian : body inscribes plot and counterplot; it is text and con/text. In the economy of substitution, transliteration, translation, where women circulate, (some)things are always lost as well as gained. I re-write my interest in equivalence: reduction and expansion. Plot and counterplot. The extra we did not control, the extra that slipped away, the bit that is missing or did not come (lack), and the uninvited guest who did, who takes us by surprise (gift). Higher mathematics.

These are issues of economy, when what was once there is no longer, when what was not there, comes, when that comes but only at this price. Like it or not, this is a form of speculation— the risky bet on a fast and substantial return. A bet on chance. Conjecture shapes capitalism. Like it or not, a lesbian's desire for a house of her own, a red Miata, a leather jacket, issues from the same source. And to write about lesbian : love is a matter of speculation—an investment, betting on a return. When you "invest" affection in your lover, what is it you are hoping for? Some interest or a small dividend. A kiss, a glance, a love letter in return?

Here I am not talking about a "value system" where we make ethical choices about our lives, as though there could be a regulatory system of absolute good (lesbian or other, if this isn't in itself a contradiction) that suggests to us that some things are "good," "better," "best." I am interested in constructing value rather than values, certain engagements, there rather than here. Perhaps the idea of an ethical practice is of interest in writing— an economy of abundance, production of value (shading, hue, tonality, nuance), "more value," regard. As Irigaray says, "We are luminous. Neither one nor two. I've never known how to

count. Up to you. In their calculations, we make two. Really,
two? Doesn't that make you laugh? An odd sort of two. And yet
not one. Especially not one. Let's leave one to them" (*This Sex*
207). The fiction of the number "one" rivals the trace covered
over in the letter "A."

A new numeracy, an/other literacy. I'm moving out of here,
away from this page, in search of my subject—writing : lesbian
energetics. How energy is transformed into tales of lesbian passion. Ex-stasy, the libidinal record of the letter presents itself in
the resonances of the words we speak to one another. Language
sparks. We can feel it in Derrida's description of how it works:
"Language is neither prohibition nor transgression, it compels
the two endlessly" (*Grammatology* 267). Prolongations, intensi-
fications, in the f(r)ictional economies of sound and sens(ation).

Like lesbian : writing, I move faster and faster, expanding
over time. I fill the bedroom, the hall. I press against the windows. I pull the arcing light of your star toward me, into me. My
gravity is inescapable.

I begin to spin, faster and faster, pulling in my luminous
spiraling arms toward the radiant center, like a skater rotating
on ice, catching you up in the glittery galactic swirl. I spin and
spin and spin, throwing off dust made reflective by your light—
pinks, greens, yellows, reds, purples—a Milky Way, a southern
aurora, across the dark vaulted sky of the bedroom. Words were
never so beautiful.

X X O X X

(CITEMENT

I think that the only "dark continent" is the one that lies
beneath the surface of language (the skin that covers it over,
masks and smooths "it" out). Language is like a skin, both on the
side of the body and out-side of the body, between the body and
the world, but also of the body, in the world.

Writing offers rough drafts for loving. It provides blueprints,
the steps marked off, itineraries for the thrill of transgression.

The perpetual separation of me from you is the *always already* of spacing, the interval pacing our harmonics, the gap that is jumped in the combustion of lesbian : energetics. Sending and receiving depend on the space between. Spacing, as we know, makessensemakingpossible. The way we traverse this interval in the chain of separation/substitution marks the human and produces its literatures. It is the originary accident, as well, that separates and conjoins me—the reader—you—the writer; the differences that allow this and every other writing to be read, to be able to (ac)count for (like re-counting or deciding what counts) what happens from the interval constituting the beginning—the letter A or in this (ac)count the letter L—to that other momentous fiction, the ending: how a "then" follows the "if." Somehow we are supposed to find our sentence here, conferred through the "lastness" of this chapter.

Dreaming: A Revision

I had a dream in which I was allowed to try to rewrite my failures with previous lesbian : lovers. The first attempt failed again. I saw my lover, now twenty-five years later, wearing the same brown coat I remember her in. We were at a big street party. I asked her to dance, but she said, "No, thanks. See you again some time." (As though this weren't a capricious dream, and we lived on the same block.) Then the second lover, who was never really my lover except in what compels and preoccupies thought and motivates the letter (we corresponded every day for more than a year, as if every letter were a kiss) appeared to me. She was wearing her old colors, maroon and black, and was still beautiful. She told me to forget my first lover (who had been my second lover in real life). For the first time, in this dream, we kissed each other. I pushed her down on the bed in her room. I was tentative but not too tentative (the cause of our failure years ago). This time she said I could kiss her, before I even mentioned it, asked for it in a way that had never been possible thirty years ago in Ann Arbor.

The release that followed the kiss, the revising of our "affair," woke me up. Now there are other chapters I can begin to rewrite. This must be what is referred to as "setting one's affairs in order."

WANNA)

I say that I want you.

(But I know the less *said* about desire the better, since we always get it wrong. That age-old problem of satisfaction; that is, getting it. So, I say, go for it, right or wrong. Something is better than nothing, isn't it? Economy again.)

We fuck. You are a charged body. I am your electromagnetic field. We spin in our orbit of space-time.

LOVING IT, DOING IT, FLAUNTING IT.

We blaze.

(DO IT

Next, the Big Bang, opaque matter, a concentrated glow, then like galaxies in a primordial universe, the energy diffuses, the temperature drops. How many thousands of years will it take for us to materialize? Energy-matter-energy-matter, and vice versa.

Energetics. We shift from level to level. We gleam in the red glow of quanta, exciting one and then the other. We move, exchanging charges in an avalanche of exhilaration. We hum. My excitement for you throbs in my ears. (My life begins to imitate art. Lesbian : writing provides the lexicon, the pre-texts and texts, of lesbian : eroticism.) I get with the beat.

RHYTHM

Pure Sex, or Rendezvous at Nick's: A Riff

They were outrageous. They looked at each other and started to drip. They sat across the table, locked in deep throat looks at

each other. They groaned and sighed, rubbed their feet together
under the table, inserted their toes into each other's crotch.
They picked over their fried chicken and lima beans, choked
down the cornbread, and planned their next minutes, orches-
trated their next moves, their sexual rhythms:

L L L L
L L L L
L L L L
L L L L
L L L L
L L L L
L L L L
L L L L
L L L L
L L L L
L L L L L L L L L L L L L
L L L L L L L L L L L L L
L L L L L L L L L L L L L

The question of love is like the question of a story's profluence: how to keep this thing going once it's set in motion. The
lover strays from the line and in irregular riffs marks out new
chains of sound. The relation of the colon, as in lesbian : writing,
marks a connection, a double play. It breaks and joins, a discon-
nective connective. All rhythm flows from there, two points that
are one in space. But what about the tempo? How fast, how
slow, do we go from here? Sometimes we speak to each other
with our hands through a rare and beautiful grammar. Our
fingers fly.

PLAY)

The letter seeks to connect me with its sense, its sender
(whoever that is). It makes me want to take (up) a position, to

"strike a pose." But I am thinking of another Madonna. No Pieta her(e). I want to uncover my/your brute instinct.

I could say that these are all wayward or purloined letters, never quite making their way from sender to receiver, stolen or lost, the message never quite what it was thought or meant to be. Sometimes their destinations change; they are sent to obscure places, other readers, without my knowing it. (In some cases, not only is the address unfamiliar, but the addressee—you, dear L—could be said to be unknown, or at least obscure.) The fact that I cannot own these letters leaves more room for doubt as to their meaning. Sometimes their meanings precede the letters, or follow me. These letters concern lesbian anarchists—sexual : textual freewheelers. Rather than Occupant or Resident, they should address the lesbian : reader. Dear Reader,

Dear L,

Tonight I can see my orgasm. A man on a horse wearing a cape and a hat, up in high chaparral country. A mountain meadow in the spring, still full of snow, with the hills banking it, encircling us. This is a vision, not a fantasy. He comes to me, or is it a woman, an uninvited participant in our s(c)ene. With me, but never looking.

Despite the wordless sounds of ecstasy, the scene is always silent, peaceful despite the frenzy of sex, the figure silhouetted, his/her features undiscernible, the vision framed. My orgasm takes me here.

This is my dream, but it is soon supplanted with another in which you star. Ready now? The next scene begins to take shape —the silken blindfold, the fur-lined cuffs with studs, the collar. . . . Now I wonder who you would rather be?

Love,
L

(PLAY IT AGAIN

"How many more than two are there."
                    —Gertrude Stein, *A Novel of Thank You*

What, for us, might be the future tense of lesbian : love? My cunt is a gateway to the future. Orgasm = intergalactic travel. In the observatory of lesbian : love, our bodies pulsate. We could say that we will burn with the brilliance of the century's supernova, outshining everything else, our luminosity an interstellar reference point for tens of thousands of years to come, visible by night and by day. Lodestars.

MORE.
   HARDER.
      FASTER.
REPEAT.
MORE.
   HARDER.
      FASTER.
AGAIN.
AND AGAIN AND AGAIN AND AND AND AND AND AND.

(I've known from the beginning that this is what my book is all about.)

Dear L,

Through writing I call out the lesbian in me, and in you as you read my letters. Space is opened, between me and the "I" (of) writing, the discursive subject, between the "I" on the page and the reader's "I," or how/who I imagine her to be. Of course, you can decide to read or to put the book down. You agree or disagree, defining a lesbian reader as you go. Together, we create templates, texts, for lesbian : love.

The most amazing thing has happened since the first chapter of this book was published. Queer people have already begun to send me letters. One sent by a gay man in Chicago contained a beautiful photograph of a statue, a boy against an elaborate drape with enormous red and yellow lilies on it. There are red, purple and yellow peppers and some eggplants tucked in and around the s(c)ene. The letter writer said:

Dear Prof. Meese: I walked into Scenes, a coffee shop in Chicago, carrying you inside like a concealed weapon, inside a book called LESBIAN TEXTS AND CONTEXTS. . . .

I admire your nerve to bring up and in your lover in a letter in the middle of your theorizing thesis about lesbian writing a new law for them/our/selves. . . .

As this letter I am now writing you on mother's day of all days (Gertrude would be proud) shows: I believe in indirect affection. I sent this letter to you and your lover to say I was affected by your writing and have affections for both of you.

Cheers from Chi Town,
Jon-Henri Damski

Also enclosed two auto-graphed photos of/by my friend. . . . He/we believe art should be given away, or it becomes a dead-give-a-way that you are not an artist, but a dealer in commodities.

It's rare to receive gifts, but both this letter and the photos live up to the strictest definition. It makes me understand how my book might be a gift, too. If enough people send me letters, perhaps I can collect them. Writing produces more writing. This story of lesbian : love starts and starts again. No contract compels its profluence, directs its desire, specifies its ending or that it ever end. It breaks open at will. A surprise gift yields other gifts. Why don't you write me when you get a chance. Then you'll understand what a "lesbian" is, the secret involved in writing : lesbian—"(. . . . . .)." I'm hoping for a reply. (A loveletter would be nice.)

Yours,
L

Dear Elizabeth,
Your face looks so remarkable when you're writing
Love,
Sandy

Notes and Letters

Notes

Chapter 1: *Theorizing Lesbian : Writing*

1. The question of the similarities and differences between Derrida, Wittig, Brossard, and Guattari/Deleuze with respect to polysexuality, "woman," and "lesbian" affords such a complex field of convergence and divergence that it deserves an extended essay devoted to its exploration.

2. See Annie Leclerc's "La lettre d'amour" in *La venue à l'écriture*, pp. 117–52.

Chapter 2: *When Virginia Looked at Vita*

1. In "The Match in the Crocus," Judith Roof observes that "the representation of the lesbian is an open site for the play of sexual difference in its relationship to the perception and representation of sexuality. Conscious of a kind of phallic preeminence, women writers are faced with the difficulty of representing perceptions unaccounted for in a phallic economy in terms of that economy" (109).

2. In this essay I advance no claims to offering a "new interpretation" of *Orlando* or of the relationship between Woolf and Sackville-West; rather, I am seeking a different expression of critical perspective and meaning. This essay departs from previous criticism because of my insistence on reading the lesbian text of Woolf and Sackville-West in terms of the lesbian text of my own experience, in terms, that is, of my own lesbian : desire and the lesbian love letter.

   I am, of course, indebted to previous scholarship on Woolf and desire; it makes this writing possible. The following works have been particularly useful to me: Louise DeSalvo, "Lighting the Cave:

The Relationship between Vita Sackville-West and Virginia Woolf,"
Signs 8, 2 (Winter 1982): 195–214; Sonya Rudikoff, "How Many
Lovers Had Virginia Woolf?" *Hudson Review* 32, 4 (Winter 1979):
54–66; Joanne Trautmann, *The Jessamy Brides* (University Park:
Pennsylvania State University Press, 1973), and especially Sherron
E. Knopf, " 'If I Saw You Would You Kiss Me?': Sapphism and the
Subversiveness of Virgina Woolf's *Orlando*," *PMLA* 103 (1988): 24–
34. Finally, critics considering Virginia Woolf owe much to Jane
Marcus's pioneering and persistent work, as do students of desire
to Linda Kauffman's *Discourses of Desire*.

3. For discussions of Woolf's "letters," see Leaska's introduction to
The Letters of Vita Sackville-West to Virginia Woolf and Catharine
Stimpson's "The Female Sociograph: The Theater of Virginia Woolf's
Letters."

4. See Jacqueline Rose, *Sexuality and the Field of Vision*, pp. 167–83,
on the question of narcissism.

5. In chapters seven and eight (pp. 138–87) of *Virginia Woolf and the
Languages of Patriarchy*, Jane Marcus traces the repressed lesbian
narrative of Woolf's relation to other lesbian writers who were her
contemporaries, and offers an insightful analysis of lesbian interests
in Woolf's texts, particularly in *A Room of One's Own*. See Marcus's observations (pp. 152, 169) concerning lesbian coding in the
Chloe and Olivia passage.

Chapter 3: A Crisis of Style

1. In "Feminisms Wake," Elaine Marks offers a provocative critique
of Faderman's assessment of Vivien, pp. 103ff.

2. In a move that parallels those of Showalter and Kolodny with
respect to works by black writers, and Toril Moi on black and
lesbian feminist theory, Zimmerman curiously excludes lesbian s/m
fiction from her study. She says in a footnote, "Some readers may
feel that I have not paid adequate attention to sadomasochistic
fiction, especially since the issue has been so divisive within the
lesbian feminist community, and the literature has proliferated in
the second half of the 1980s. I believe that this literature needs a
serious and dispassionate study of its own, one that would place it
within the historical tradition of libertine and pornographic literature, as well as lesbian literature, and that would take on the

difficult question of differentiating between pornography and erotica" (249 n. 31).

3. See Marcus's discussion of Barnes's substitution of O'Connor's "nonphallic penis" for the "symbolic phallus as law" (228–29).

4. Gerstenberger is not alone in her resistance to classifying Barnes as a lesbian writer. Jane Marcus, in "Laughing at Leviticus," makes a parallel gesture, arguing that "the status of *Nightwood* as a lesbian novel or a cult text of high modernism has obscured the ways in which it is a French novel" (222), but at the same time Marcus discusses its lesbian content in original and compelling ways.

5. While our perspectives are rather different on this point, Shari Benstock offers an interesting reading of "Robin Vote's tragedy" as "the impossibility of her becoming a subject of her own discourse" (263).

Chapter 4: Gertrude Stein and Me

1. The difficulties the contemporary reader might have with Stein concerning her positions on race and class are certainly worth exploring, since matters are far from conclusive. See, for example, Richard Wright's letter to Stein (*Flowers* 379–81), in which he discusses his sense of indebtedness to her and the success of his own writing—a matter that must be taken into account in arguments about the co-optation of black material (specifically in "Melanctha") by white writers. Wright's own position also deserves careful scrutiny. Similarly, Stein's relationships to Bernard Fay and Marshal Petain with respect to collaboration and the Vichy government in World War II need thorough consideration. These complex issues merit judicious analysis rather than hasty judgments in one direction or another.

Sonia Saldivar-Hull, in "Wrestling Your Ally," offers the kind of probing analysis that these matters deserve; particularly striking is her discussion of feminist suppression or neglect of Bridgman's discussion from over thirty years ago of Stein's racism in "Melanctha." Still, Saldivar-Hull's essay produces some of its own problems too: the question of when a stereotype is not a stereotype, who is free to make particular kinds of observations and who is not (194–95); McKay's unremarked comments that Melanctha could be "a Jewess," and Jeff Campbell a "type of white lover described by a colored woman" (190); and, finally, the unexamined value of the concept of canonicity, that is, how the canon by definition works by inclusions and exclusions that suggest its limits.

2. There are a number of commentators on Stein's lesbianism who offer much less-qualified assessments of her accomplishments, and thus stand as exceptions, most notable among them Judy Grahn, Cynthia Secor, and Rebecca Mark. See also Rachel Blau DuPlessis's "Woolfenstein" for a probing analysis of the relation between these two writers in the context of experimentalism.

3. Shari Benstock opens her discussion of Stein and Toklas by situating them historically; see p. 143.

4. See Stimpson's "The Mind, the Body, and Gertrude Stein," for an extended discussion of *Q.E.D.* and the circumstance surrounding it.

5. Friedman and Fuchs present a compelling argument concerning the relative neglect of female experimentalists.

6. William Gass is among those who remark upon the radical significance of Stein's work in her time: "that in fifteen years [after *Tender Buttons*] *The Well of Loneliness*, genteel, inept, and as unlibidinous as beets, will still cause a scandal; that the Dadaists haven't uttered their first da yet, let alone their second" (158).

7. See Carolyn Burke's discussion of sisters and lovers, "Gertrude Stein," pp. 236–37.

8. For a most interesting interpretive account of *Ida*, see Schmitz, pp. 226–39.

9. Lisa Ruddick, in *Reading Gertrude Stein*, makes an excellent case for the development of Stein style in relation to her influences and sexual choice.

10. I am borrowing this lov(h)er from another revolutionary lesbian writer, Nicole Brossard, and her English translator Barbara Goddard.

11. Secor points out in "*Ida*, A Great American Novel" that Stein's use of the continuous present is "her solution to the problem of having been born a female artist whose only tradition is a patriarchal one" (99). Ruddick gives a very curious reading of Stein's repetition in *The Making of Americans* as anal erotic stylistics, pp. 55–136.

12. See JoAnn Loulan's analysis of lesbian responses to butch and femme in *The Lesbian Erotic Dance*, esp. pp. 29–30.

13. Chessman's keen differentiation between Ida's "yes" and Molly

Bloom's "yes" (193–94) is worth reviewing: "Whereas Molly's monologue concludes with a double consummation of male quester(s) with female object of desire, and of past moment with present, *Ida* resists both conclusion and consummation" (193).

14. Jayne Walker notes that *The Making of Americans* resists the characteristics of the Barthesian text of pleasure, resembling more closely the text of bliss (184).

Chapter 5: Lesbian (Sem)Erotics

1. Austin eventually "abandons the statement/performance opposition" because he takes into account "the subversive, and self-subversive, potential of the performative" (Felman 63–64).

2. See for example Daniel Rancour-Laferriere's discussion of the language of obscenities, pp. 222–27.

3. See Monique Wittig on the lesbian as outside the sex/gender system, "One Is Not Born a Woman," esp. pp. 52–53.

4. See DeLauretis's explanation of (in)difference as a term of heterosexual discourse (156).

5. For an excellent discussion of metaphor, consult Patricia Parker's *Literary Fat Ladies*, esp. pp. 12–52.

6. See Brossard, *Surfaces of Sense*, and Wittig, *Les Guérillères*.

Chapter 6: X-Rated

1. "The Feminist Sexuality Debates" presents a variety of perspectives on feminist treatments of sexuality and the implications for lesbianism. See also "Sex Resistance in Heterosexual Arrangements" by A Southern Women's Writing Collective [WAS].

2. Thanks are due to Vonceil Smith for discussions concerning selective silences within the lesbian community.

3. Williams, pp. 209–18, offers a fuller analysis of the question of identification.

4. See Butler's discussion of the subject position in fantasy, "The Force of Fantasy," 109–10.

5. See Thaïs E. Morgan's response (114–15) to Kappeler's representation of pornography's "master plot."

6. Butler presents a brilliant analysis of the Helms position and related issues in "Force."

7. Susan Suleiman, in *Subversive Intent*, pp. 72–87, presents an excellent discussion of Andrea Dworkin's reading of Bataille's pornographic text, *Histoire de l'oeil* (*Story of the Eye*). Yingling's discussion of feminist opposition to pornography ("How" 6) is also worth consulting.

8. Shirley Nelson Garner points out that, in *Lesbian Psychologies: Explorations and Challenges*, "no contributor to the collection is a medical doctor or describes herself as a psychoanalyst" (179–80).

9. Margaret Nichols's essays on the effects of conformity, or diminishing difference and lesbian sexual arousal are interesting in this respect.

References

Adams, Parveen. "Of Female Bondage." In *Between Feminism and Psychoanalysis.* Ed. Teresa Brennan, 247–65. London and New York: Routledge, 1989.

Against Sadomasochism: A Radical Feminist Analysis. Ed. Robin Ruth Linden, Darlene R. Pagano, Diana E. H. Russell, and Susan Leigh Star. San Francisco: Frog in the Well, 1982.

Allen, Carolyn. "Writing toward *Nightwood:* Djuna Barnes' Seduction Stories." In *Silence and Power: A Reevaluation of Djuna Barnes.* Ed. Mary Lynn Broe, 54–65. Carbondale and Edwardsville: Southern Illinois University Press, 1991.

Anzaldua, Gloria. *Borderlands/La Frontera: The New Mestiza.* San Francisco: Spinsters/Aunt Lute, 1987.

Barnes, Djuna. *Ladies Almanack.* New York: Harper and Row, 1972.

———. *Nightwood.* New York: New Directions, 1961.

Bar On, Bat-Ami. "Feminism and Sadomasochism: Self Critical Notes." In *Against Sadomasochism: A Radical Feminist Analysis.* Ed. Robin Ruth Linden, Darlene R. Pagano, Diana E. H. Russell, and Susan Leigh Star, 72–82. San Francisco: Frog in the Well, 1982.

Barreno, Maria, Maria Teresa Horta, and Maria Velho da Costa. *The Three Marias: New Portuguese Letters.* Trans. Helen R. Lane. New York: Bantam, 1976.

Barthes, Roland. *The Pleasure of the Text.* Trans. Richard Miller. New York: Hill and Wang, 1975.

Bataille, Georges. *L'Érotisme.* Paris: UGE, Coll. 10/18, 1965.

Benstock, Shari. *Women of the Left Bank: Paris, 1900–1940.* Austin: University of Texas Press, 1986.

Berry, Ellen E. "On Reading Gertrude Stein." *Genders,* no. 5 (1989): 1–20.

Birtha, Becky. "Plumstone." In *By Word of Mouth: Lesbians Write the*

Erotic. Ed. Lee Fleming. Charlottetown, Prince Edward Island: Gynergy, 1989.

Bowlby, Rachel. *Virginia Woolf: Feminist Destinations.* Oxford: Blackwell, 1988.

Bridgman, Richard. *Gertrude Stein in Pieces.* New York: Oxford University Press, 1970.

Bright, Susie. *Susie Sexpert's Lesbian Sex World.* Pittsburgh and San Francisco: Cleis Press, 1990.

Brophy, Brigid. *In Transit.* London: GMP Publisher Ltd., 1969.

Brossard, Nicole. *The Aerial Letter.* Trans. Marlene Wildeman. Toronto: Women's Press, 1988.

———. *L'Amer ou Le chapître effrité: théorie/fiction.* Montreal: L'Hexagone, 1977.

———. "Djuna Barnes: De Profil Moderne." In *Mon héroine,* 189–214. Montreal: Les Editions du remue-menage, 1981.

———. *Lovhers.* Trans. Barbara Godard. Montreal: Guernica Editions, 1986.

———. *Sous la langue/Under Tongue.* Montreal: Gynergy Books, 1987.

———. *Surfaces of Sense.* Trans. Fiona Strachan. Quebec: Coach House Press, 1989.

———. *These Our Mothers: Or: The Disintegrating Chapter.* Trans. Barbara Godard. Quebec: Coach House Quebec Translations, 1983.

Broumas, Olga. *Beginning with O.* New Haven and London: Yale University Press, 1977.

———. *Perpetua.* Port Townsend, Wash.: Copper Canyon Press, 1989.

Burke, Carolyn. " 'Accidental Aloofness': Barnes, Loy, and Modernism." In *Silence and Power: A Reevaluation of Djuna Barnes.* Ed. Mary Lynn Broe, 67–79. Carbondale and Edwardsville: Southern Illinois University Press, 1991.

———. "Gertrude Stein, the Cone Sisters, and the Puzzle of Female Friendship." In *Writing and Sexual Difference.* Ed. Elizabeth Abel, 221–42. Chicago: University of Chicago Press, 1982.

Butler, Judith. "The Force of Fantasy: Feminism, Mapplethorpe, and Discursive Excess." *difference* 2 (1990): 105–25.

———. *Gender Trouble: Feminism and the Subversion of Identity.* New York and London: Routledge, 1990.

Califia, Pat. *Doc and Fluff: The Distopian Tale of a Girl and Her Biker.* Boston: Alyson Pubs., 1990.

———. *Macho Sluts.* Boston: Alyson Pubs., 1988.

Carter, Angela. *The Sadeian Woman and the Ideology of Pornography.* New York: Pantheon, 1978.

Causse, Michèle. "L'Interloquée." Trans. Susanne de Lotbinière-Harwood. *Trivia* 13 (Fall 1988): 79–90.

———. *Lesbiana: Seven Portraits.* Paris: Le Nouveau Commerce, 1980.

———. "Le monde comme volonté et comme représentation." *Vlasta*, no. 1 (1983): 10–25.

Chessman, Harriet Scott. *The Public Is Invited to Dance: Representation, the Body, and Dialogue in Gertrude Stein.* Stanford, Calif.: Stanford University Press, 1989.

Cixous, Hélène. "Rethinking Differences: An Interview." Trans. Isabelle de Courtivron. In *Homosexualities and French Literature: Cultural Contexts/Critical Texts.* Ed. George Stambolian and Elaine Marks, 70–86. Ithaca, N.Y., and London: Cornell University Press, 1979.

Cixous, Hélène, Madeleine Gagnon, and Annie Leclerc. *La venue à l'écriture.* Paris: Union Générale d'Editions, 1977.

Cole, Susan G. "A View from Another Country." In *The Sexual Liberals and the Attack on Feminism.* Ed. Dorchen Leidholdt and Janice C. Raymond, 191–97. New York: Pergamon Press, 1990.

Cook, Blanche Wiesen. " 'Women alone stir my imagination': Lesbianism and Cultural Tradition." *Signs* 4 (1979): 718–39.

Daly, Mary. *Gyn/Ecology: The Metaethics of Radical Feminism.* Boston: Beacon Press, 1978.

Daly, Mary, and Jane Caputi. *Webster's First New Intergalactic Wickedary of the English Language.* Boston: Beacon Press, 1987.

Defromont, Françoise. *Virginia Woolf: Vers la maison de lumière.* Paris: Editions des femmes, 1985.

De Lauretis, Teresa. "Sexual Indifference and Lesbian Representation." *Theatre Journal* 40 (1988): 155–77.

Deleuze, Gilles, and Felix Guattari. *Anti-Oedipus: Capitalism and Schizophrenia.* Trans. Robert Hurley et al. New York: Viking, 1972.

Derrida, Jacques. *Dissemination.* Trans. Barbara Johnson. Chicago: University of Chicago Press, 1981.

———. *The Ear of the Other: Otobiography, Transference, Translation.* Ed. Christie V. McDonald. Trans. Peggy Kamuf. New York: Schocken, 1985.

———. *Margins of Philosophy.* Trans. Alan Bass. Chicago: University of Chicago Press, 1982.

Derrida, Jacques. *Of Grammatology*. Trans. Gayatri Chakravorty Spivak. Baltimore and London: Johns Hopkins University Press, 1976.
———. *The Post Card: From Socrates to Freud and Beyond*. Trans. Alan Bass. Chicago and London: University of Chicago Press, 1987.
———. "Sending: On Representation." *Social Research* 49 (1982): 294–326.
———. "Women in the Beehive: A Seminar with Jacques Derrida." In *Men in Feminism*. Ed. Alice Jardine and Paul Smith, 189–203. New York: Methuen, 1987.
Derrida, Jacques, and Christie V. McDonald. "Choreographies." *Diacritics* 12 (1982): 66–76.
Diamond, Irene, and Lee Quinby. "American Feminism in the Age of the Body." *Signs* 10 (1984): 119–25.
DiBattista, Maria. *Virginia Woolf's Major Novels: The Fables of Anon.* New Haven: Yale University Press, 1980.
Dolan, Jill. "The Dynamics of Desire: Sexuality and Gender in Pornography and Performance." *Theatre Journal* 39 (1987): 156–74.
DuPlessis, Rachel Blau. "Woolfenstein." In *Breaking the Sequence: Women's Experimental Fiction*. Ed. Ellen G. Friedman and Miriam Fuchs, 99–114. Princeton, N.J.: Princeton University Press, 1989.
———. *Writing beyond the Ending: Narrative Strategies of Twentieth-Century Women Writers*. Bloomington: Indiana University Press, 1985.
Engelbrecht, Penelope J. " 'Lifting Belly Is a Language': The Postmodern Lesbian Subject." *Feminist Studies* 16 (1990): 85–114.
Faderman, Lillian. *Surpassing the Love of Men: Romantic Friendship and Love Between Women from the Renaissance to the Present*. New York: William Morrow, 1981.
Felman, Shoshana. *The Literary Speech Act: Don Juan with J. L. Austin, or Seduction in Two Languages*. Trans. Catherine Porter. Ithaca, N.Y.: Cornell University Press, 1983.
"The Feminist Sexuality Debates." Estelle B. Freedman, Barrie Thorne, et al. *Signs* 10 (1984): 102–35.
Field, Andrew. *Djuna: The Life and Times of Djuna Barnes*. New York: Putnam's, 1983.
Fifer, Elizabeth. "Is Flesh Advisable? The Interior Theater of Gertrude Stein." *Signs* 4 (1979): 472–83.
Flowers of Friendship: Letters Written to Gertrude Stein. Ed. Donald Gallup. New York: Knopf, 1953.

Fox-Genovese, Elizabeth. *Feminism Without Illusions: A Critique of Individualism*. Chapel Hill and London: University of North Carolina Press, 1991.

Frank, Joseph. *The Widening Gyre: Crisis and Mastery in Modern Literature*. New Brunswick, N.J.: Rutgers University Press, 1963.

Freud, Sigmund. *Beyond the Pleasure Principle*. Trans. and ed. James Strachey. New York and London: W. W. Norton, 1961.

Friedman, Ellen G., and Miriam Fuchs. "Contexts and Continuities: An Introduction to Women's Experimental Fiction in English." In *Breaking the Sequence: Women's Experimental Fiction*. Ed. Ellen G. Friedman and Miriam Fuchs, 3–51. Princeton, N.J.: Princeton University Press, 1989.

Gallop, Jane. *Thinking Through the Body*. New York: Columbia University Press, 1988.

Garner, Shirley Nelson. "Feminism, Psychoanalysis, and the Heterosexual Imperative." In *Feminism and Psychoanalysis*. Ed. Richard Feldstein and Judith Roof, 164–81. Ithaca, N.Y., and London: Cornell University Press, 1989.

Gasché, Rodolphe. "*Ecce Homo* or the Written Body." *Oxford Literary Review* 7 (1985): 3–24.

Gass, William H. "Gertrude Stein and the Geography of the Sentence: 'Tender Buttons.' " In *Gertrude Stein*. Ed. Harold Bloom, 145–63. New York: Chelsea House, 1986.

Gerstenberger, Donna. "The Radical Narrative of Djuna Barnes's *Nightwood*." In *Breaking the Sequence: Women's Experimental Fiction*. Ed. Ellen G. Friedman and Miriam Fuchs, 129–39. Princeton, N.J.: Princeton University Press, 1989.

Gilbert, Sandra M., and Susan Gubar. *No Man's Land: The Place of the Woman Writer in the Twentieth Century*, vol. 2, *Sexchanges*. New Haven and London: Yale University Press, 1989.

Glendinning, Victoria. *Vita: A Life of V. Sackville-West*. New York: Knopf, 1983.

Gould, Karen. *Writing in the Feminine: Feminism and Experimental Writing in Quebec*. Carbondale and Edwardsville: Southern Illinois University Press, 1990.

Grahn, Judy. *Really Reading Gertrude Stein: A Selected Anthology with Essays by Judy Grahn*. Freedom, Calif.: Crossing Press, 1989.

Greenberg, David F. *The Construction of Homosexuality*. Chicago and London: University of Chicago Press, 1988.

Grover, Jan Zita. "Words to lust by." *Women's Review of Books* 7.2 (November 1990): 21–23.

Guattari, Felix. "A Liberation of Desire." Interview by George Stambolian. Trans. G. Stambolian. In *Homosexualities and French Literature: Cultural Contexts/Critical Texts.* Ed. George Stambolian and Elaine Marks, 56–69. Ithaca, N.Y., and London: Cornell University Press, 1979.

Heath, Stephen. *The Sexual Fix.* London and Basingstoke, U.K.: Macmillan Press Ltd., 1982.

Hoff, Joan. "Why Is There No History of Pornography?" In *For Adult Users Only: The Dilemma of Violent Pornography.* Ed. Susan Gubar and Joan Hoff, 17–46. Bloomington and Indianapolis: Indiana University Press, 1989.

Holman, C. Hugh, and William Harmon. *A Handbook to Literature.* New York: Macmillan, 1986.

Hubbard, Stacy Carson. "Me, Myself and *Ida:* Stein's Self-Conjugations." Unpublished paper presented at MLA, December 1989.

Irigaray, Luce. *Speculum of the Other Woman.* Trans. Gillian C. Gill. Ithaca, N.Y.: Cornell University Press, 1985.

———. *This Sex Which Is Not One.* Trans. Catherine Porter. Ithaca, N.Y.: Cornell University Press, 1985.

Jeffreys, Sheila. "Sado-Masochism: The Erotic Cult of Fascism." *Lesbian Ethics* 2 (1986): 65–82.

———. "Sexology and Antifeminism." In *The Sexual Liberals and the Attack on Feminism.* Ed. Dorchen Leidholdt and Janice C. Raymond, 14–27. New York: Pergamon Press, 1990.

Kaite, Berkeley. "Reading the Body Textual: Fetish Relations in Soft and Hard Core." *Semiotics* 6 (1989): 79–93.

Kamuf, Peggy. *Signature Pieces: On the Institution of Authorship.* Ithaca, N.Y., and London: Cornell University Press, 1988.

Kannenstine, Louis F. *The Art of Djuna Barnes: Duality and Damnation.* New York: New York University Press, 1977.

Kappeler, Susanne. *The Pornography of Representation.* Minneapolis: University of Minnesota Press, 1986.

Kauffman, Linda S. *Discourses of Desire: Gender, Genre, and Epistolary Fiction.* Ithaca, N.Y., and London: Cornell University Press, 1986.

Kiss and Tell. "Drawing the Line." OUT/LOOK, no. 10 (1990): 6–11.

Knopp, Sherron E. " 'If I Saw You Would You Kiss Me?': Sapphism and the Subversiveness of Virginia Woolf's *Orlando*." *PMLA* 103 (1988): 24–34.

Lacan, Jacques. *Écrits: A Selection*. Trans. Alan Sheridan. New York: W. W. Norton, 1977.

———. "Intervention on Transference." *Feminine Sexuality: Jacques Lacan and the école freudienne*. Ed. Juliet Mitchell and Jacqueline Rose, 61–73. New York and London: W. W. Norton, 1982.

———. *The Seminar of Jacques Lacan*. Ed. Jacques Alain Miller. Book I: *Freud's Papers on Technique, 1953–1954*. Trans. John Forrester. New York and London: W. W. Norton, 1988.

———. *The Seminar of Jacques Lacan*. Book II: *The Ego in Freud's Theory and in the Technique of Psychoanalysis, 1954–1955*. Trans. Sylvana Tomaselli. New York and London: W. W. Norton, 1988.

Lanser, Susan Sniader. "Speaking in Tongues: *Ladies Almanack* and the Discourse of Desire." In *Silence and Power: A Reevaluation of Djuna Barnes*. Ed. Mary Lynn Broe, 156–68. Carbondale and Edwardsville: Southern Illinois University Press, 1991.

Leaska, Mitchell A. "Introduction." In *The Letters of Vita Sackville-West to Virginia Woolf*. Ed. Louise DeSalvo and Mitchell A. Leaska, 11–46. New York: William Morrow, 1985.

Lederer, Laura, ed. *Take Back the Night: Women in Pornography*. New York: Morrow, 1980.

Lee, Judith. "*Nightwood*: 'The Sweetest Lie.' " In *Silence and Power: A Reevaluation of Djuna Barnes*. Ed. Mary Lynn Broe, 207–18. Carbondale and Edwardsville: Southern Illinois University Press, 1991.

LeMasters, Carol. "S/M and the Violence of Desire." *Trivia* 15 (1989): 17–30.

Lesbian Nuns: Breaking Silence. Ed. Rosemary Curb and Nancy Manahan. Tallahassee, Fla.: Naiad Press, 1985.

Lesselier, Claudie. "Social Categorizations and Construction of a Lesbian Subject." Trans. Mary Jo Lakeland. *Feminist Issues* 7 (1987): 89–94.

Lorde, Audre. *Sister Outsider: Essays and Speeches*. Trumansburg, N.Y.: Crossing Press, 1984.

———. *Zami: A New Spelling of My Name*. Trumansburg, N.Y.: Crossing Press, 1982.

Loulan, JoAnn, with Sherry Thomas. *The Lesbian Erotic Dance: Butch Femme Androgyny and Other Rhythms*. San Francisco: Spinsters Book Co., 1990.

MacKinnon, Catharine A. "Liberalism and the Death of Feminism." In *The Sexual Liberals and the Attack on Feminism*. Ed. Dorchen Leidholdt and Janice C. Raymond, 3–13. New York: Pergamon Press, 1990.

Mapplethorpe, Robert (with Richard Marshall). *Robert Mapplethorpe*. New York: Whitney Museum and Little Brown, 1988.

Maraini, Dacia. *Letters to Marina*. Trans. Dick Kitto and Elspeth Spottiswood. Freedom, Calif.: Crossing Press, 1987.

Marcus, Jane. "Laughing at Leviticus: *Nightwood* as Woman's Circus Epic." In *Silence and Power: A Reevaluation of Djuna Barnes*. Ed. Mary Lynn Broe, 221–50. Carbondale and Edwardsville: Southern Illinois University Press, 1991.

———. *Virginia Woolf and the Languages of Patriarchy*. Bloomington and Indianapolis: Indiana University Press, 1987.

Mark, Rebecca, ed. "Introduction." In Gertrude Stein, *Lifting Belly*, xi–xxxiv. Tallahassee, Fla.: Naiad Press, 1989.

Marks, Elaine. "voice iv: Feminisms Wake." *boundary 2* 12 (1984): 99–110.

Marlatt, Daphne, and Nicole Brossard. *Characters/ Jeu de Lettres*. Montreal: abj writing, 1986.

Meese, Elizabeth. *Crossing the Double-Cross: The Practice of Feminist Literary Criticism*. Chapel Hill and London: University of North Carolina Press, 1986.

———. *(Ex)Tensions: Re-Figuring Feminist Criticism*. Urbana and Chicago: University of Illinois Press, 1990.

Michel, Frann. "Displacing Castration: *Nightwood, Ladies Almanack*, and Feminine Writing." *Contemporary Lit* 30 (1989): 33–58.

Minow-Pinkney, Makiko. *Virginia Woolf and the Problem of the Subject*. Brighton, U.K.: Harvester Press, 1987.

Morgan, Thaïs E. "A Whip of One's Own: Dominatrix Pornography and the Construction of a Post-Modern (Female) Subjectivity." *Semiotics* 6 (1989): 109–36.

Nestle, Joan. "The Fem Question." In *Pleasure and Danger: Exploring Female Sexuality*. Ed. Carole S. Vance, 232–41. Boston: Routledge and Kegan Paul, 1985.

———. *A Restricted Country*. Ithaca, N.Y.: Firebrand, 1987.

Nichols, Margaret. "Lesbian Sexuality: Issues and Developing Theory," and "Doing Sex Therapy with Lesbians: Bending a Heterosexual Paradigm to Fit a Gay Life-style." In *Lesbian Psychologies: Explorations and Challenges*, 97–125, 242–60. Ed. Boston Lesbian Psychologies Collective. Urbana and Chicago: University of Illinois Press, 1987.

———. "Low Sexual Desire in Lesbian Couples." In *Sexual Desire Disorders*. Ed. Sandra R. Leiblum and Raymond C. Rosen, 387–412. New York and London: Guilford Press, 1988.

Nicolson, Nigel. *Portrait of a Marriage.* New York: Athenaeum, 1973.

Nin, Anaïs. *The Diary of Anaïs Nin*, vol. 2, *1934–1939.* New York: Swallow Press and Harcourt Brace, 1967.

Pacteau, Francette. "The Impossible Referent: Representations of the Androgyne." In *Formations of Fantasy.* Ed. by Victor Burgin, James Donald and Cora Kaplan, 62–84. London and New York: Methuen, 1986.

Parker, Patricia. *Literary Fat Ladies: Rhetoric, Gender, Property.* London and New York: Methuen, 1987.

Plumb, Cheryl J. *Fancy's Craft: Art and Identity in the Early Works of Djuna Barnes.* Cranbury, N.J.: Associated University Press, 1986.

Rancour-Laferriere, Daniel. *Signs of the Flesh: An Essay on the Evolution of Hominid Sexuality.* New York: Mouton de Gruyter, 1985.

Raymond, Janice G. *A Passion for Friends: Toward a Philosophy of Female Affection.* Boston: Beacon Press, 1986.

Rian, Karen. "Sadomasochism and the Social Construction of Desire." In *Against Sadomasochism: A Radical Feminist Analysis.* Ed. Robin Ruth Linden, Darlene R. Pagano, Diana E. H. Russell, and Susan Leigh Star, 45–50. San Francisco: Frog in the Well, 1982.

Rich, Adrienne. *On Lies, Secrets, and Silence: Selected Prose 1966–1978.* New York: W. W. Norton, 1979.

Ricoeur, Paul. *The Rule of Metaphor: Multi-disciplinary Studies of the Creation of Meaning in Language.* Trans. Robert Czerny et al. Toronto and Buffalo: University of Toronto Press, 1977.

Rochefort, Christiane. "The Privilege of Consciousness: An Interview by Cecile Arsene." Trans. Marilyn Schuster. In *Homosexualities and French Literature: Cultural Contexts/Critical Texts.* Ed. George Stambolian and Elaine Marks, 101–13. Ithaca, N.Y., and London: Cornell University Press, 1979.

Rogers, W. G. *When This You See Remember Me*. New York: Avon, 1948.

Roof, Judith. *A Lure of Knowledge: Lesbian Sexuality and Theory*. New York: Columbia University Press, 1991.

———. "The Match in the Crocus: Representations of Lesbian Sexuality." In *Discontented Discourses: Feminism/Textual Intervention/Psychoanalysis*. Ed. Marleen S. Barr and Richard Feldstein, 100–16. Urbana and Chicago: University of Illinois Press, 1989.

Rose, Jacqueline. *Sexuality in the Field of Vision*. London: Verso, 1986.

Ross, Andrew. *No Respect: Intellectuals & Popular Culture*. New York and London: Routledge, 1989.

Rubin, Gayle. "The Leather Menace: Comments on Politics and S/M." In *Coming to Power: Writings and Graphics on Lesbian S/M*, 194–229. Boston: Alyson Publications, 1987.

Ruddick, Lisa. *Reading Gertrude Stein: Body, Text, Gnosis*. Ithaca, N.Y., and London: Cornell University Press, 1990.

Sackville-West, Vita. *The Letters of Vita Sackville-West to Virginia Woolf*. Ed. Louise DeSalvo and Mitchell A. Leaska. New York: William Morrow, 1985.

———. *Seducers in Ecuador and The Heir*. London: Virago Press, 1987.

Saldivar-Hull, Sonia. "Wrestling Your Ally: Stein, Racism, and Feminist Critical Practice." In *Women's Writing in Exile*, ed. Mary Lynn Broe and Angela Ingram, 181–98. Chapel Hill and London: University of North Carolina Press, 1989.

Schmitz, Neil. *Of Huck and Alice: Humorous Writing in American Literature*. Minneapolis: University of Minnesota Press, 1983.

Scott, James B. *Djuna Barnes*. Boston: G. K. Hall, 1976.

Secor, Cynthia. "Can We Call Gertrude Stein a Non-Declared Lesbian Writer?" Unpublished manuscript, 1979.

———. "*Ida*, A Great American Novel." *Twentieth Century Literature* 24 (1978): 96–107.

Sherwood Anderson/Gertrude Stein: Correspondence and Personal Essays. Ed. Ray Lewis White. Chapel Hill: University of North Carolina Press, 1972.

Showalter, Elaine. "Critical Cross-Dressing: Male Feminists and the Woman of the Year." In *Men in Feminism*. Ed. Alice Jardine and Paul Smith, 116–32. New York: Methuen, 1987.

Sight Specific: Lesbians & Representation. Ed. Lynne Fernie, Dinah Forbes, and Joyce Mason. Toronto: Printer's Ink, 1988.

Silence and Power: A Reevaluation of Djuna Barnes. Ed. Mary Lynne Broe. Carbondale and Edwardsville: Southern Illinois University Press, 1991.

Sischy, Ingrid. "A Society Artist." In Robert Mapplethorpe (with Richard Marshall), *Robert Mapplethorpe*, 76–88. New York: Whitney Museum and Little Brown, 1988.

Smith, Barbara. "Toward a Black Feminist Criticism." In *The New Feminist Criticism: Essays on Women, Literature, and Theory.* Ed. Elaine Showalter, 168–85. New York: Pantheon, 1985.

Soble, Alan. *Pornography: Marxism, Feminism, and the Future of Sexuality.* New Haven, Conn., and London: Yale University Press, 1986.

Sontag, Susan. "The Pornographic Imagination." In *Styles of Radical Will*, 35–73. New York: Dell, 1969.

Southern Women's Writing Collective. "Sex Resistance in Heterosexual Arrangements." In *The Sexual Liberals and the Attack on Feminism*, 140–47. Ed. Dorchen Leidholdt and Janice C. Raymond. New York: Pergamon Press, 1990.

Stein, Gertrude. *Everybody's Autobiography.* New York: Random House, 1973.

———. *Geography and Plays.* 1922; rpt. New York: Something Else Press, 1968.

———. *How To Write.* Preface and Introduction by Patricia Meyerowitz. New York: Dover, 1975.

———. "Ida." In *How Writing Is Written.* Ed. Robert Bartlett Haas, 43–47. Los Angeles: Black Sparrow Press, 1974.

———. *Ida: A Novel.* New York: Random House, 1941.

———. *Lectures in America.* New York: Random House, 1935.

———. "Lend a Hand or Four Religions." In *Useful Knowledge.* Foreword by Edward Burns; introduction by Keith Waldrop. Barrytown, N.Y.: Station Hill Press, 1988.

———. *Lifting Belly.* Ed. Rebecca Mark. Tallahassee, Fla.: Naiad Press, 1989.

———. *"Two: Gertrude Stein and Her Brother" and Other Early Portraits (1908–1912).* New Haven: Yale University Press, 1951.

———. *Wars I Have Seen.* New York: Random House, 1945.

Stein, Gertrude. *What Are Masterpieces?* Ed. Robert Bartlett Haas. New York: Pitman, 1970.

Stimpson, Catharine R. "The Female Sociograph: The Theater of Virginia Woolf's Letters." In *The Female Autograph.* Ed. Domna C. Stanton and Jeanine Parisier Plottel, 193–203. New York: New York Literary Forum, 1984.

———. "Gertrude Stein and the Transposition of Gender." In *The Poetics of Gender*, 1–18. Ed. Nancy K. Miller. New York: Columbia University Press, 1986.

———. "The Mind, the Body, and Gertrude Stein." *Critical Inquiry* 3 (1977): 489–506.

———. "The Somograms of Gertrude Stein." In *The Female Body in Western Culture*, 30–43. Ed. Susan Suleiman. 1986.

———. *Where the Meanings Are: Feminism and Cultural Spaces.* New York: Methuen, 1988.

———. "Zero Degree Deviancy: The Lesbian Novel in English." *Critical Inquiry* 8 (1981): 363–79.

Suleiman, Susan Rubin. *Subversive Intent: Gender, Politics and the Avant-Garde.* Cambridge, Mass.: Harvard University Press, 1990.

Trautmann, Joanne. *The Jessamy Brides: The Friendship of Virginia Woolf and V. Sackville-West.* University Park: Pennsylvania State University Press, 1973.

Valverde, Mariana. "Beyond Gender Dangers and Private Pleasures: Theory and Ethics in the Sex Debates." *Feminist Studies* 15 (1989): 237–54.

Vance, Carole S. "Pleasure and Danger: Toward a Politics of Sexuality." In *Pleasure and Danger: Exploring Female Sexuality*, 1–27. Boston: Routledge and Kegan Paul, 1984.

Walker, Jayne L. "History as Repetition: 'The Making of Americans.'" In *Gertrude Stein.* Ed. Harold Bloom, 177–99. New York: Chelsea House, 1986.

Williams, Linda. *Hard Core: Power, Pleasure, and the "Frenzy of the Visible."* Berkeley and Los Angeles: University of California Press, 1989.

Willis, Ellen. "Feminism, Moralism, and Pornography." In *Powers of Desire: The Politics of Sexuality.* Ed. Ann Snitow, Christine Stansell, and Sharon Thompson, 460–67. New York: Monthly Review Press, 1983.

Wittig, Monique. *Les Guérillères*. Trans. David Le Vay. Boston: Beacon Press, 1985.

———. *The Lesbian Body*. Trans. David Le Vay. New York: William Morrow and Co., 1975.

———. "The Mark of Gender." *Feminist Issues* 5 (1985): 3–12.

———. "One Is Not Born a Woman." *Feminist Issues* 1 (1981): 47–54.

———. "Paradigm." Trans. George Stambolian. *Homosexualities and French Literature: Cultural Contexts/Critical Texts.* Ed. George Stambolian and Elaine Marks, 114–21. Ithaca, N.Y., and London: Cornell University Press 1979.

———. "The Point of View: Universal or Particular." *Feminist Issues* 3 (1983): 63–69.

Wittig, Monique, and Sande Zeig. *Lesbian Peoples: Material for a Dictionary.* New York: Avon, 1979.

Woolf, Virginia. *The Diary of Virginia Woolf*, vol. 3, *1925–1930*. Ed. Anne Olivier Bell and Andrew McNeillie. New York: Harcourt Brace Jovanovich, 1980.

———. *Flush: A Biography.* New York: Harcourt, Brace and World, 1933.

———. *The Letters of Virginia Woolf*, vol. 3, *1923–1928*. Ed. Nigel Nicolson and Joanne Trautmann. New York and London: Harcourt Brace Jovanovich, 1977.

———. *Orlando: A Biography.* Harcourt Brace Jovanovich, 1956.

———. *A Writer's Diary* [*WD*]. Ed. Leonard Woolf. New York: Harcourt Brace Jovanovich, 1953.

Yingling, Thomas E. *Hart Crane and the Homosexual Text: New Thresholds, New Anatomies.* Chicago and London: University of Chicago Press, 1990.

———. "How the Eye Is Caste: Robert Mapplethorpe and the Limits of Controversy." *Discourse* 12 (1990): 3–28.

Zimmerman, Bonnie. *The Safe Sea of Women: Lesbian Fiction, 1969–1989.* Boston: Beacon Press, 1990.

Index